Reconfiguring Europe

British Studies in Applied Linguistics

Published in collaboration with British Association for Applied Linguistics (BAAL)

Each volume in the series consists of a selection of peer-reviewed papers on a theme of general interest, based on presentations at the BAAL Annual General Meetings. In covering state-of-the-art research in the UK and elsewhere, the series aims to broaden the scope of applied linguistics to include areas as diverse as sociolinguistics, discourse analysis, communication studies and language education.

Volumes 1-15 in this series were published by Multilingual Matters; volumes 16-18 were published by Continuum.

For more information about BAAL visit their website: www.baal.org.uk

Previously published
Applied Linguistics at the Interface
Edited by Mike Baynham, Alice Deignan and Goodith White
(Volume 19)

British Studies in Applied Linguistics: Volume 20

Reconfiguring Europe

The contribution of applied linguistics

Selected papers from the
Annual Meeting of the British Association for Applied Linguistics
King's College, London, September 2004

Edited by
Constant Leung and Jennifer Jenkins

BRITISH ASSOCIATION FOR APPLIED LINGUISTICS

in association with

LONDON   OAKVILLE

Published by

Equinox Publishing Ltd.
UK: Unit 6, The Village, 101 Amies Street, London, SW11 2JW
USA: DBBC, 28 Main Street, Oakville, CT 06779
www.equinoxpub.com

First published 2006

British Library Cataloguing-in-Publication Data
A catalogue record for this book is available from the British Library.

ISBN-10 1 84553 090 X   (paperback)
ISBN-13 978 184553 090 7   (paperback)

Library of Congress Cataloging-in-Publication Data
Reconfiguring Europe : the contribution of applied linguistics / edited
by Constant Leung and Jennifer Jenkins.
    p. cm. -- (British studies in applied linguistics ; v. 20)
 Includes bibliographical references.
 ISBN 1-84553-090-X (pbk.)
1. Multilingualism--Europe. 2. Pluralism (Social sciences)--Europe.
3. Language policy--Europe. 4. English language--Political
aspects--Europe. 5. European Union. 6. Europe--Politics and
government--1989- I. Leung, Constant, 1950- II. Jenkins, Jennifer,
1950- III. British studies in applied linguistics ; 20.
 P115.5.E85R46 2006
 306.44'6094--dc22

                                    2006004274

Typeset by Catchline, Milton Keynes (www.catchline.com)
Printed and bound in Great Britain by Antony Rowe Ltd.,
Chippenham, Wiltshire

Contents

Contents

1   Introduction

Constant Leung and Jennifer Jenkins

King's College London

Europe has a multilingual population, and events such as the European Year of Languages (2001) signal that multilingualism is a desired social goal at a policy level. However, as the 2004 BAAL conference and this collection show, there is a good deal about the extent and nature of this multilingualism that is little understood, let alone enacted in legislation and institutional practices. So in that sense, multilingualism comes across to some extent as a form of policy rhetoric without substance.

As an association, BAAL has been aware for some time that within the broad domain of applied linguistics, there has been a considerable amount of energy and effort expended on a range of issues relating to the study of language policy, language use and language education with a European focus. Thematically the 2004 conference was dedicated to exploring the multifaceted language and linguistic issues facing Europe today. Therefore it was gratifying to see that scholars from a range of international contexts came together to discuss these issues. The keynote speakers of the 2004 conference examined some of the most critical questions of our time.

In the first paper, Arturo Tosi draws attention to multilingualism in relation to the official EU community languages in the legislative arena, and demonstrates the extent of the marginalisation of multilingualism that occurs. Member states are entitled to have official documents made available in the official languages of the EU. However, in practice, as Tosi points out, the translation process appears to have little regard of the ways in which meaning is constructed within individual languages in highly socially and culturally sensitive ways. The result is a near-automated translation approach which produces texts with distorted meanings, thus making the ideal of multilingualism little more than a mere formality.

Guus Extra provides a useful and detailed account of the realities of multilingualism in a number of European communities. His focus, however, is on a more comprehensive concept of 'community' languages than is usually adopted in policy discussions, one which embraces not only the official EU languages but also all other languages used in the home. He thus alerts us to multilingualism of a different kind, i.e. local community-based multilingualism involving often under-represented and almost invisible languages such as Turkish and Romani. This is another kind of marginalisation of multilingualism. Julia Sallabank explores these issues in relation to one specific case of an 'invisible' language. By means of a rigorous examination of the merits of reviving and maintaining Guernesiais she provides a telling example of the value of promoting local multilingual vitality.

Robert Phillipson also supports the ideal of a multilingual Europe, but picks up on the theme of the historically significant ascendancy of English in Europe and its impact on other languages. If there is to be a European *lingua franca*, it should not, he argues, give advantages to native speakers of that language over speakers with other mother tongues. He gives tentative approval to the notion of English as a *Lingua Franca* (ELF) (see his critique of House in his paper). On the other hand, unlike Phillipson, Juliane House is entirely comfortable with the notion of English as a European *lingua franca*. She considers it to be *sui generis*, able to accommodate a multiplicity of norms and voices but at the same time to involve the emergence of new ELF norms. The Phillipson and House arguments show the kinds of contribution applied linguistics can make in articulating the pivotal role the English language, as a rapidly expanding *lingua franca*, has in shaping an increasingly mobile communication landscape in a Europe that is also conscious of the value of linguistic diversity.

With the two papers which follow, by Pascaline Scalone and Brian Street, and by Martina Möllering, we turn to educational considerations. Scalone and Street examine the notion of academic language with reference to ethnolinguistic minority students. They question the conventional assumptions regarding the concepts of 'discourse community' and 'academic genre'. They show that in the London context, itself part of the wider Europe, multiplicity should be a standard consideration. By contrast, Möllering provides an account of how specialist language teaching material for academic purposes can be developed by systematic exploitation of the use of dedicated corpora, in this case, German ancient history texts.

In the final two papers, those of Monika Bednarek and Natalie Braber, we remain with corpus approaches. In the first, Bednarek examines the evaluative standpoints on European issues shown by a number of British newspapers, and observes that a systematic investigation based on clear criteria can reveal social values expressed in the print media. Braber, on the other hand, takes a wider view of language corpus by examining the changes and neologisms in the German language since unification in 1989, showing that many of the social tensions and emerging issues are reflected in its lexicon.

We would like to thank the members of the BAAL Executive Committee and the local organising committee for the enthusiasm and hard work that made the 2004 conference such a stimulating occasion for discussion and exchange of views. We would also like to thank all the postgraduate students at King's College London who gave up valuable time to provide organisational help over the three conference days. Finally, our thanks to all the conference speakers and participants for their contribution. We feel that the conference was very successful in drawing much-needed and long overdue attention to issues of immense importance for language policy and practice in the Europe of the twenty-first century.

2   The devil in the kaleidoscope: can Europe speak with a single voice in many languages? [1]

Arturo Tosi

Abstract

I would like to address the question raised in the subtitle: can Europe speak with a single voice in many languages? In the course of my presentation I shall attempt to answer the question from a linguistic point of view. This doesn't mean that I am not aware of the political side of the problem: the problem of a Europe that cannot speak with a single voice because of a lack of consensus. It is simply that I have more to say about multilingualism. In upholding the values of a multilingual Europe I shall return to some linguistic situations that are becoming increasingly important in contemporary Europe; and, in particular, language contact and language transfer, interlanguage and error analysis. I should like to do this in memory of the scholarship of Pitt Corder, to whom this lecture is dedicated. In my conclusions, I intend to suggest a possible new direction for applied linguistics to promote the preservation of language and culture diversity. I hope this will be a useful contribution to our conference which is devoted to the role of linguistic research in the reconfiguration of Europe. But now, without further ado, let me begin by introducing a notion that is central to most of the issues I have just mentioned: I speak of the devil of course!

Survival of a linguistic mosaic

In the first half of the last century the German philologist Gherhardt Rohlfs (1892–1986) who dedicated his whole career to the history of the many tongues spoken in the South of Italy, conducted a thorough language survey in Calabria, a large region in the Southwest of Italy. Rohlfs was trying to identify the origin and the variations of three diverse languages within that region – Neapolitan, Sicilian and Calabrian. These three Romance languages, together with a variety of Greek language which had, he said, been imported in pre-Roman times, were spoken in small speech communities, most of which were in isolated mountain areas, while a few were scattered along the coasts of the Ionic and Tyrrhenian seas. In his survey he used a significant selection of key words that could be representative of diverse local cultures, ethnic traditions and religious beliefs. One of these words was 'devil', for which Rohlfs identified as many as 34 variants within Calabria. In the first half of the twentieth century, Calabria was still wholly uncontaminated by any industrial development or urban influence. It was quite well known for its rich oral literature, which resulted from a wealth of local customs, faiths, fears and beliefs, some of which were clearly pre-Christian or pagan in origin.

Rohlf analysed these 34 and classified them into categories representing different local traditions. In his findings we can see, *caronte* – the Charon of Greek mythology; *berzabuccu*, an Old Testament Hebrew word for Beelzebub; *satinazzu*, from a Hebrew word for Satan, which probably came via Greek and which means the demon who plots against God. Then we have *farfariellu* and *farfarieddu*, personifications of an evil spirit, whose names are from the Arabic word *farfar*, meaning goblin. Then we find *lucifer* and *lucifaru* and other variants *capucifaru*, *cifaru* and *zifaru*, creatures who are burning and showing light in the night, from Latin of course. Then *bruttu* and *brutta bestia* (ugly beast) and *pintu* and *pintissimu*, the beast that looks red, very red. And *ciancu*, *sciancu*, *zoppieddu*, a beast with a limp. Also *dimmoniu*, again from Greek, meaning evil spirit and *diavulu*, or *rijavulu*, also from old Greek meaning the enemy, and *nomicho*, also meaning enemy, from the Latin root *non amicus*; and *majidittu* meaning cursed by God.

Probably the most interesting in Rohlfs' (1975) list is the word *mahametta*, that is to say 'Mohammed', founder and symbol of Islam. It is not surprising that this is a synonym for 'devil' in communities that withdrew from the coast and took refuge in the mountains to escape the raids of the pirates from the sea. In the view of these communities, the Turkish pirates of Islamic faith were obviously inspired by the evil spirit of their God. That is what Christians were led to believe at the time, which reminds us of how little history has taught some of our politicians and how much it still has to teach them.

Rohlfs' study demonstrates why, and how, multilingualism in Italy had survived almost intact, when compared to most European countries. Had Italy been unified under the Medici family in the fifteenth century, Florentine would probably have become the national language, i.e. at the same time as political unification and linguistic stabilisation took place in most other European nations. Instead, Italy was unified in 1861, and the total number of native speakers of Florentine, from then on known as Italian, amounted to 2.5%, although some 10% were in contact with that language. All the other inhabitants of the Peninsula, many of whom lived in rural communities, had different mother tongues. They spoke other Romance languages, which were not dialects of Florentine, the *lingua franca* which eventually became the national language.

For 100 years after political unification the spread of the national language remained slow and patchy. Not even the Fascist regime, with its 20 years of nationalist policies that banned all dialects and minority languages, had any significant effect on the spread of the national language. It was only later, after the Second World War and the birth of democratic Italy, that a common language spread in an unprecedented way. This happened when the isolation of rural communities was broken down, and their linguistic conservatism became challenged by new factors. This is why we say that the linguistic situation of the Italian Peninsula has experienced more changes in the last 50 years than in the previous 500. First, there was an economic transformation. In 1961 the majority of Italians were still employed in agriculture and only a minority in industry or in service industries. In the 1960s the situation rapidly altered and the trend was reversed. Second, there was an increase in internal mobility. One direction of migration was from the rural South to the industrialised North. The other was due to the urbanisation that took place in all regions, from rural areas to small towns or large cities. Third, there were the new powerful media of communication. The Fascist regime was quick to appropriate the technical innovations of the radio, the newspapers and the film industry, once it realised that communication via the new media could exercise great influence on people's attitudes and beliefs. But this policy did not succeed in imposing a new language alien to most people. It was only with a television in each household that Italian speakers achieved levels of linguistic homogenisation and lexical standardisation that were without precedent.

Language death

The adoption of a common language and the abandonment of local community languages involved a process that is well captured by Fishman's (1966) assessment of language change in an immigration context. He asserts that the shift is completed after three generations: that is to say after a bilingual generation had mediated between one generation monolingual in the old language, and the other monolingual in the new. In Italy this massive language shift was welcomed by the literary and educated circles, but the less articulate voices of Italian society were not so enthusiastic. Let us listen to the words of Ignazio Buttitta (1899–1997), a Sicilian poet. He used to compose verses in his native language, verses he himself recited to other shepherds during the long winter nights in the mountains, or to his co-villagers gathered in the piazza after the Sunday fair.

A un populu,	*You may clap a people in irons,*
mittici i catini, spugghiatilu	*strip it bare,*
attuppatici a vucca,	*gag it,*
ed è ancora libiru	*it will still be free.*
Livatici u travagghiu	*You may take away its work,*
u passaportu	*its passport,*
u lettu unni dormi	*the bed where it sleeps,*
a tavula unni mancia	*the table where it eats:*
ed è ancora riccu	*it will still be rich.*
Un populu,	*A people,*
diventa poviru e servu,	*becomes poor and enslaved*
quannu ci arrobanu a lingua	*when they rob it of the language*
addutata di patri,	*passed down by its fathers,*
a perdi pi sempri.	*and it is lost for ever.*
Diventa poviru e servu,	*It becomes poor and enslaved*
quannu i paroli non figghianu paroli	*when words no longer give birth to words*
e si manciano tra d'iddi.	*and they eat each other out of house and home.*
Mi nn'addugnu ora,	*I realise it now,*
mentri accordu a chitarra du dialettu,	*as I tune the guitar of my 'dialettu'*
ca perdi na corda lu jornu.	*which each day loses another string.*
Mentri arripezzu a tila camulata,	*While I mend the threadbare cloth,*
chi tissèru i nostri avi	*once woven by our ancestors*
cu lana di pecuri siciliani.	*with the wool of Sicilian sheep.*
E sugnu poviru:	*And I am poor,*
haiu i dinari, e non li pozzu spènniri;	*I have money I cannot spend,*
i gioielli, e non li pozzu rigalari;	*jewels I cannot give as presents,*
u cantu	*my song,*
nta gaggia	*but I sit in a cage*
cu l'ali tagghiati.	*with my wings clipped.*
Un poviru,	*A poor man,*
chi chianci e non cummuovi;	*who weeps without touching anyone's heart*
chi giuisci e non è cridutu.	*who rejoices without being understood.*
Un poviru,	*A wretched soul,*
c'addatta nte minni strippi	*who takes suck from the breasts*
da matri putativa,	*of a foster parent,*
chi u chiama figghiu.	*who calls him her son.*
Nuàtri l'avevamu a matri,	*We had a mother*
nni l'arrubaru;	*who was snatched from us;*
aveva I minni a funtana di latti	*she had breasts, a fountain of milk,*
e ci vippiru tutti,	*at which all took nourishment*
ora ci sputanu.	*but now they spit on her.*
Nni ristò a vuci d'idda,	*What she left us is her voice,*

a cadenza,	*her intonation,*
a mutivu stunatu;	*the lilting discord;*
a nota vascia	*the deep resonance*
du sonu e du lamentu;	*in our words and laments:*
chiss, non nni ponnu rubari.	*these cannot be taken away.*
Nni risto a sumiglianza,	*We have kept her looks,*
l'andatura,	*her gait,*
i gesti,	*her gestures,*
u focu di l'occhi!	*the fire in her eyes,*
chissi, non nni ponnu rubari.	*these cannot be taken away.*
Non nni ponnu rubari,	*They cannot rob us of these,*
ma ristamu poviri e orfani u stissu.	*but we are poor orphans nonetheless.*

(Translation by Roger Griffin)

The language of Ignazio Buttitta's verses (1972) is emotional, angry, strong, lyrical and beautiful. In sociolinguistics the notions he expresses are referred to as 'language contact' and 'language shift', 'standardisation' and 'stigmatisation', 'language and identity' and, of course, 'language death'. Should I continue along this road? Won't the conclusions waiting for me seem already too obvious? Let me try to summarise them. Multilingualism within Italy has never been official, or supported by a national policy. By contrast, multilingualism in Europe today is official, and Europe does not have, and is very unlikely to have, a policy of a common language, or a *lingua franca*, at least in the near future. But there are other considerations too. The official language of Italy spread neither by promotion, nor by the coercion exercised by the authoritarian Fascist regime. It spread as soon as it found a consensus instrumental to consolidating its socio-economically hegemonic position. This dilemma is very well known in sociolinguistics, as we are reminded of the words of another much quoted linguist who has written extensively on the survival of minority languages in the United States. I quote Bernard Spolsky: 'to salvage a language and to salvage its speakers is not the same thing' (1972).

Limits of a common European language

For this reason many people feel that the unofficial but increasingly hegemonic role of English, as a *lingua franca* is, despite the EU official policy of multilingualism, a serious threat to national languages and multilingualism in Europe. Others argue against this gloomy perspective. They see that our rich cultural and linguistic diversity is based on strong national identities and these, at least today, do not seem to be even remotely challenged by a supranational identity that might require the adoption of a common language. These two positions have been summarised by Umberto Eco in his book *The Search for the Perfect Language*. Eco published this work in 1993, the symbolic year in which the common European House was built. Here he sets out to provide a retrospective and prospective vision of the problems and solutions of living in a Europe that is divided by its many languages. At the end of 15 chapters about European and non-European experiments aimed at finding, or creating, the perfect language, a universal language capable of uniting people, Eco reaches his conclusion.

> Today more than ever before ... European culture is in urgent need of a
> common language that might heal its linguistic fractures. Yet, at the same
> time, Europe needs to remain true to its historic vocation as the continent of
> different languages...
>
> ...[F]aced with the prospect that in a future European Union the language of
> a single nation might prevail, those states with scant prospects of imposing
> their own language and which are afraid of the predominance of another one
> (and thus all states except one) might band together to support the adoption
> of an International Artificial Language

Then, after assessing the advantages and disadvantages of Esperanto, Eco concludes that:

> ...The only alternative is to discover a natural language which is so 'perfect'
> (so flexible and powerful) as to serve as a tertium comparationis. (Which
> might allow us to shift from an expression in language A to an expression
> in language B by deciding that both are equivalent to an expression of a
> metalanguage C. If such tertium comparationis really existed, it would be
> a perfect language; if it did not exist, it would remain a mere postulate on
> which every translation ought to depend.)

Eco says that the solution can be found in Ayamara, a language that is still spoken by indigenous people living between Bolivia and Peru. He explains that this language is a unique natural idiom, in that it displays an immense flexibility, for example, in accommodating neologisms, and is therefore capable of expressing many subtleties which other languages can only capture through complex circumlocutions. Apart from the suggestion that the adoption of Aymara could be the painless solution for multilingual Europe (is it a joke or a serious project? – the Italian semiologist and novelist prefers to leave his readers to guess), it seems to me that Eco's argument raises a fundamental issue: that of multilingual translation, as this presupposes the choice of one language in a particular situation that functions as the original for all translations.

Some linguists – who most probably know Eco more for his puzzling novels than for his vision on European multilingualism – have already seen the relevance of the interaction between English and other languages. I found one paper on English as an International Language particularly enlightening as it makes a distinction between 'real English' and 'Realistic English'. In this paper, by Barbara Seidlhofer (2003), we read:

> Sociolinguistic research indicates that if – and this is a vital condition – English is appropriated by its users in such a way as to serve its unique function as EIL (English as an International Language) it does not constitute a threat to other languages but, precisely because of its delimited role and distinct status, leaves other languages intact.

Seidlhofer also says:

> From the above considerations it follows that the most crucial concern must be to understand how 'English' functions in relation to other languages.

In the situation of languages in contact described by Seidlhofer, the question of how 'English' functions in relation to other languages is of course only one side of the coin. The other side, how 'other languages function in relation to English' is the one I am more concerned with here, and I think the issue can best be illustrated, perhaps paradoxically, by the sentence 'Europe must speak with a single voice in many languages' once we attempt a translation into some other European languages.[2] Let's take Italian for example. As you know, the slogan 'Europe must speak with a single voice in many languages' was introduced in 2001, the Year of Languages, to promote awareness of multilingualism throughout Europe. As I have the good fortune to teach in England and also in Italy, I asked my Italian undergraduates to translate the English version of the slogan into Italian, and I collected from my group of some 100 students no fewer than 30 different renderings. What are the lessons we can learn from for this experiment in translation?

The challenges of multilingual translation

One lesson is that the Italian language has a very flexible word order. This characteristic, coupled with the very high number of quasi-synonymic nominal variations (with only slightly different semantic connotations) means that Italian is not a highly standardised language. This feature is often described as the 'vagueness' of Italian, a characteristic that is represented by the peculiar meaning of the word *vago*, which in Italian means also 'lovely', 'attractive', 'poetic' (Calvino, 1984). Indeed Italian translators are well aware that this vagueness can increase the scope for translation of works of literature, but in non-literary texts vagueness is a distinct disadvantage.

The second point we can note is that the word *voce*, in Italian, normally refers only to the sound of language or the tone of the speaker, never to the content of the speech. Many of my students, all native Italian speakers, felt unhappy with a literal translation of the slogan and attempted to rephrase it by way of a circumlocution.

The third point is the most intriguing in that none of the 30-odd renderings given by my native speakers was the same as that of the official translation provided by the Translation Service in Brussels when they published the Italian version of the slogan. What happened was that EU translators, too, were unhappy about the semantic difference between the word *voce* in Italian and 'voice' in English, but they found a different solution. Their solution reads:

L'Europa deve parlare all'unisono in lingue diverse

And the notion *all'unisono* was chosen, most probably, because it appeared in the French version of the slogan, where *unisson*, is an acceptable translation, because it defines 'unity of sentiments and voices', in other words 'unanimously' in addition to that of 'unity of the sound made by musical instruments'.

But this semantic extension is not reflected in Italian. Thus the disturbing tendency to alternate between English and French (as the original language for other translations) raises some fundamental questions about multilingual translation in the EU – the choice of the original, the translation system and the role of translators (Tosi, 2002a). Let us begin with the first issue.

The choice of the original

In the European Parliament all languages can be used as working languages, and can be either source or target languages, depending on the circumstances. This means that when the Union had 11 languages (up to May 2004) the Parliament Translation System needed to cope with 110 combinations – each language functioning as the source for the other ten. Since this policy of full multilingualism has been applied to the recent enlargements, 380 combinations for 20 languages are required. The Union is considering admitting other countries, including more from eastern Europe. Every time the Union grows, so does the number of translators and interpreters from the new official languages. The justification for this massive operation of simultaneous interpretation was that, when European MPs interact within the assemblies and committees, they are speaking for the electors in the national community that they represent. The Commission has adopted a system of multilingualism with an unequal, rather than equal, status among the official languages. Only English and French are working languages. The justification was that this was more practical, and it would not interfere with the multilingual operations of the institution. Yet since the Commission's institutional task is to serve and inform the public, European citizens must receive all documentary and legislative materials in their national languages.

There are two main points to note about these arrangements. The first point is that the Commission, by limiting the combinations and reducing the problem of quantity, has introduced a problem regarding quality. This will not be easy to solve, since an increasing number of EU officials are not native speakers of English. And today English is, effectively, the only *lingua franca*, as French tends to be used exclusively for internal staff regulations and the management of the Commission offices.

The second point is that if interpreters give impromptu oral translations in the Parliament, those in the EU who really set models and affect linguistic trends are the translators of written language, because their choices are seen by the general public. They are the true innovators in this new multilingual environment, where changes are adopted in writing long before they have been accepted in the spoken language. And this is certainly one unprecedented outcome of language contact in Europe today.

The translation system

Multilingual translation in the EU has now reached massive proportions. Not only must the EU legislation be published in all the member states' official languages before it becomes national law, but the Parliament and the Commission translate draft consultative papers, working documents and other publications on most topics of social, political and economic interest for the general public, and all these are fed into gigantic memory banks. All European citizens must be able to read and understand documents and legislation in their own languages, according to the 1958 Language Charter which remains the legal basis for the EU multilingual policy. Thus, from the very beginning of the process of European integration, it was decided that the official languages would be those (initially four in number) of the member states. This principle is enshrined in Regulation 1 of the 1958 Charter, which is amended each time a new country joins the EU so as to include the new language. Today the Regulation reads:

> legislation and other documents of general application shall be **drafted** [my emphasis] in the 20 official languages…

The term 'drafted' in the Charter suggests that the legislator should operate with parallel and simultaneous draftings in all the languages. Indeed, this was the case in the early years. But over time this was gradually changed, and an administrative reform introduced a system whereby a single language version was always to be the starting-point for the production of the other versions by way of translation. The multilingual transactions today have reached such quantitative and qualitative proportions that, for many reasons the system leaves a lot to be desired. Accordingly, the text given to Italian translators, for example, may not be the original version (English), but itself a translation (French or Spanish) functioning as a 'bridge' between the source and the target language.

The role of translators

There are three issues. First, the EU's translation procedures have not been devised or analysed by language experts. Rather, some of its major operations were introduced as routine decisions as if they were to have no impact on the policy nor on the quality of the end-product. Second, in legal terms, translation was introduced in lieu of multilingual drafting, and it is an integral part of the Community legislative process, but is officially absent from the legislation itself. Third, since translation is not seen to 'exist' as an issue in the legislative process, the translators are 'invisible'. It is interesting that some of the keenest promoters of a review of the translation system in EU institutions are the translators themselves (Correia, 2002). This paradox accounts for two more controversial decisions: (1) the separation of the translation service from the decision making divisions, and (2) the anonymous and collective (rather than individual) responsibility of translators.

As far as EU multilingual policy is concerned, the notion of 'equivalence' is crucial. For example, the various language versions of the regulations and other European laws are 'equivalent', in the etymological sense of the word, since they have the same legal value and can be invoked indiscriminately by EU citizens irrespective of their member state of origin or the country's official language. Yet two assumptions need to be tested. One assumption is that legal equivalence is supported by textual equivalence, without which there cannot be equality of the message for all European citizens. The second is that all translations must be as readily accessible as the originals. Otherwise EU citizens are not 'equal' as regards the messages they receive. It is crucial, therefore, that translators find the best linguistic choices in order to safeguard the 'equivalence' of documents and legislative materials, as these must carry the same legal value in all language versions. But translators are not encouraged to act as mediators between the intentions of the writers and the effect of the translations on the readers. Quite the contrary, the rather 'mechanistic' procedures they are trained to adopt encourage the straightfoward substitution of all items in a text, and the direct transfer of its format and punctuation, from one language to another. Sometimes separate sections of a text (all in one source language) are given to different translators. At other times, the sections to be translated are in different source languages, and are given to different translators (Koskinen, 2002).

Languages in contact with and without speaker interaction

In sum, the multilingual system, which is in operation in the largest translation agency in the world, actually leads translators to believe that all translations are acceptable and equal, as long as the single units in their texts are replaced one by one, and if care is taken to ensure that the units in the new language correspond to those from the source language. This visual approach is extended to all textual features, from the graphic lay-out, to the typographical style, including the length of the sentences and the punctuation. The result is an impressive visual correspondence; but this surface approach clashes with the linguistic anomalies of the texts and the semantic discrepancies between the different language versions. In my view the best visual representation for this multilingual system is the emblem of the kaleidoscope: the multifaceted structure inside the cylinder reflects a constellation of words on its multitude of mirrors. The cylinder is a self-organising system, where every word has an equivalent, every language is a sum of its parts, and the kaleidoscope multiplies these parts by means of the phantasmagoric play of mirrors. Every time a new language is admitted, a new mirror is inserted in the kaleidoscope, and a new word will be reflected.

In the past the outcome of language contact was determined by international relations between cultural élites or by the movements of migrant populations, which brought large communities of speakers of different languages into contact. In both cases our European languages have been enriched by these exchanges; possibly because the interaction between the two cultures in contact always involved interaction between speakers. Today the rapid development of communication and information technologies, together with the internationalisation of our exchanges, has introduced the challenge of an unprecedented volume of international loan-word traffic. But the growing role of technology in the multilingual communication between the EU and its citizens shows how these exponentially increased opportunities for language contacts can take place with little, if any, cultural interaction between the communities of speakers concerned.

Before the computer revolution, European translators dictated their translations into a dictaphone or directly to a typist. In the mid-1990s all translators were equipped with their own computer, and each individual PC was connected to a centralised database, which allowed past translations and other documents to be consulted and retrieved directly from a server. This memory system, which is now ten years old, is called *workbenches*. It enables users not only to search translation memories for previously translated sentences, but also gives them access to databases for individual terms. Any text for translation that contains passages or key ideas which have been translated in the past can be consulted, and adapted directly from the main EU server at the touch of a button, and can be recreated by simply copying old passages into the new translation by an automatic system of cutting and pasting. It seems to me that the workbenches innovation will have dramatic consequences not only for international communication, but also in that it automates the process of language change and language standardisation in national contexts. I shall mention just three new developments.

First, the translation memory may well irreversibly validate the linguistic forms of old ideas, and new concepts, without any human interaction. This is the case when the choices made at the click of a mouse by translators operating under horrible time pressures become final solutions, once they are memorised by the workbenches. Second, the traditional distinction between the written and the spoken word is becoming increasingly blurred. This is because new EU ideas are coming to depend on the written language of translation rather than on the language spoken within national communities. Third, the workbenches will make it difficult, if not impossible, for speakers in the national communities to participate in the process of standardisation. All proposals for decisions, directives and regulations may be available on the Internet for everybody to read, judge and react to, but it is most unlikely that anyone will succeed in challenging the validation of the choices made by a translator's terminal, once they are put in cyberspace to feed a memory for years to come.

Does my criticism of the system of multilingual translation arise from an allergy to modern technologies, or from the hypersensitivity of a language scholar who wishes to preserve the integrity of his mother tongue and resist all changes ? I hope not. Italian, which for historical reasons is still not highly standardised, could be more exposed than other languages to this new trend, but I have found similar patterns in most languages, although there are reasons why some are more prone to Europeanisation than others. Certainly English and French, which have coexisted for many years as working languages within the EU institutions, have benefited from resources and opportunities for transparency and standardisation which are unrivalled by any other language. For English and French, the problem may be one of purism as we can see in this letter published in the newspaper *Le Monde* (27 June 1998):

Why, if not for laziness, should we restrict (deform?) the meaning of the French mondialisation or, more precisely planetarisation, perfectly fit for the bill? Warped by this new meaning, globalisation is an Anglicism and introduces an ambiguity (an unnecessary polysemy) into our language, thus making it poorer, not richer. Vive la 'mondialisation'!

In Britain, too, some of the media condemn or even ridicule EU deviations from 'proper' standard British use. But many people would say that, in Britain, public perception of the EU's influence on language is often distorted by ideological, not linguistic, factors. You may judge for yourself from this message quoted from the 'very first Euro-birthday card' on sale in shops and newsagents in Brussels and Luxembourg, which advertises on the front 'Under new regulations, the imperial standard happy birthday has been replaced with a simplified 'Euro-greeting' [3]

...merry enjoyment of a non-specific ongoing sequential annual event or events which relate specifically to that event hereafter known as 'the event' of birth in as much as a specific time or instant of time shall be attributed to the event as previously determined in accordance with the regulations which refer to the event in question, being wholly or in part the event under discussion, to wit and pertaining to the non-specific event to which it has already been certified that contains a time reference appropriate to the yearly period which it is desirous to refer to as the event as specified above in all its exactitude and finite detail apropos the intended date reference and celebrating time.

Certainly the principle 'the closer the cultures, the closer is the translation' applies to EU materials, but there are also factors of an unprecedented nature affecting the many languages that are never used as working languages: that is to say, those that the voice of Europe is always translated into, never from. I refer to international concepts, the discourse style and culturally specific rhetoric associated with contemporary market economy, liberal politics, large-scale participation in local and regional governments. These, for example, can hardly be found in the linguistic heritage and the everyday repertoire of the new democracies from Eastern Europe which have just joined the EU. Alien notions and foreign borrowings, clearly Anglo-American in origin, may actually complicate the reception of the voice of Europe within many member states, and we do not know whether they will, or will not, exacerbate the sense of loss of linguistic identity amongst a large sector of European citizens. Should this be the case, the problem will not be one of linguistic purism or ideological prejudice: it will be one of transparency and, ultimately, of democracy.

Conclusions

Have a great number of threads been interwoven in this talk? Which thread should I pull to find the end in my hand? There is the thread of language stand-ardisation, access and participation, which I have already begun to unwind, which is beautifully summarised by this passage from *Alice's Adventures in Wonderland* (Carroll, 1865).

> 'It seems very pretty' she said when she had finished it, 'but it is rather hard to understand!' (you see she didn't like to confess even to herself, that she couldn't make it out at all). 'Somehow it seems to fill my head with ideas – only I don't exactly know what they are! However, somebody killed something! That's clear, at any rate.

But I would like to draw to an end with a quotation from a well-known Italian writer who was a brilliant translator himself: Italo Calvino. In 1965 he wrote:

> Nowadays every cultural question has immediate international resonance; it needs instantaneous verification around the globe, or at least it must be checked against a worldwide series of points of reference… Our age is characterised by this contradiction: on the one hand we need to be able to translate everything which is said into other languages immediately; on the other we realise that every language is a self-contained system of thought and by definition untranslatable… My prediction is this: each language will revolve around two poles. One pole is immediate translatability into other languages, which will come close to a sort of all-embracing, high-level interlanguage; and another pole will be where the singular and secret essence of the language, which is by definition untranslatable, is distilled. And from this distillation systems as different as popular slang and the poetic creativity of literature will drink.

Calvino also warns us about what he calls 'the great linguistic cataclysms of the next centuries', against which no language seems to have adequate defences to protect itself from the 'thrust towards antilanguage' 'not French, German, Russian, Spanish or Italian – not even English (though for different reasons)' and he adds:

> The devil today is approximation. The devil is in any discourse that is approximate or vague, and in any thought that is imprecise. The effect is heightened when approximation is accompanied by a sense of superiority and arrogance. The devil is the enemy of clarity, and can be found both internally and in relations with others. The devil is the personification of deception and self-deception. (Calvino, 1978)

To conclude, I've spoken about the unification of Italy and the integration of Europe, and I mentioned language shift by coercion and by consensus. And I also talked about the EU language policy, which is so divided between equality and utopia, and the kaleidoscope that refracts the world into mirrors and multiplies its spectral images in a countless number of languages, producing distorted simulacra of diversity and multiplicity. And I also spoke in favour of multilingualism, the value of which we must defend, together with the value of the subtleties of thought and imagination of our cultures, against the more generic, anonymous and abstract formulas of a centralised think-tank. And this is where we are today. I'm sure that we shall be able to cope with the integration of Europe, and the great linguistic changes of the next centuries, provided that we do not permit entry to what we are not prepared to accept: the devil in the kaleidoscope, for example, whose threat to European multilingualism I have tried to illustrate here today.

Notes

1 This paper is based on a presentation which formed The 2004 Pit Corder Memorial Lecture.
2 'Europe must speak with a single voice in many languages' is a slogan which was often used to promote awareness of multilingualism during the celebrations for 2001, The Year of Languages.
3 The Humour Factory, 'A funny sort of business' birthday card (The Paper House Group, Shepard, 1998).

References

Buttitta, I. (1972) *Io faccio il poeta*. Milano: Feltrinelli.
Calvino, I. (1965) L'italiano, una lingua tra le altre lingue. *Rinascita* 5, XXII, January 1965. Reprinted in *Una pietra sopra* 141–8. (1995 edition) Milano: Mondadori.
Calvino, I. (1978) Note sul linguaggio politico. First published in *Domenica del Corriere*, March 1978. Reprinted in *Una pietra sopra* 370. (1995 edition) Milano: Mondadori.
Calvino, I. (1984) *Lezioni Americane. Sei proposte per il Prossimo Millennio*. Torino: Einaudi, English translation (1988): *Six Memos for the Next Millennium*. Cambridge, MA: Harvard University Press.
Carroll, L. (1865) *Alice's Adventures in Wonderland*. London: Macmillan and Co.
Correia, R. (2002) Translation of EU legal texts. In A. Tosi (ed.) (2002b) 38–44.
Eco, U. (1993) *La ricerca della lingua perfetta*, English translation (1995) *The Search for the Perfect Language*. Oxford: Blackwell.

Fishman, J. A. (1966) *Language Loyalty in the United States*. The Hague: Mouton.

Koskinen, K. (2000) Translating in the EU Commission. *The Translator* 6(1): 49–65.

Rholfs, G. (1975) *Nuovo dizionario dialettale della Calabria*. Ravenna: Lango Editore.

Seidlhofer. B. (2003) *A Concept of International English and Related Issues*: *from 'Real English' to 'Realistic English'*? Strasbourg: Council of Europe. Language Policy Division, DG IV, Directorate of School, Out-of-School and Higher Education.

Spolsky, B. (1972) The limits of language education. In B. Spolsky (ed.) *The Language Education of Ethnic Minority Children* 193–200. Rowley, MA: Newbury House.

Tosi, A. (2002a) The Europeanisation of the Italian language by the European Union. In L. Lepschy and A. Tosi (eds) *Multilingualism in Italy: past and present* 170–94. Oxford: Legenda.

Tosi, A. (ed.) (2002b) *Crossing Barriers and Bridging Cultures: the challenge of the multilingual translation for the European Union*. Clevedon, Buffalo, Toronto, Sydney: Multilingual Matters.

3 Dealing with multilingualism in multicultural Europe: immigrant minority languages at home and school

Guus Extra

Abstract

The focus of this discussion is on the status of immigrant minority languages (henceforward IM) at home and at school from four different European perspectives. In the first section I offer discourse perspectives on the semantics and some of the central notions in this field of study. In the second part I discuss the utilisation and effects of different demographic criteria for the definition and identification of (school) population groups in a multicultural society. Next I offer sociolinguistic perspectives on the distribution and vitality of IM languages across Europe. In this context the rationale and major outcomes of the Multilingual Cities Project, carried out in six major multicultural cities in different European Union (henceforward EU) nation-states, are presented. Finally I offer comparative perspectives on educational policies and practices in the domain of IM languages in the six EU countries under discussion. I conclude with an outlook on how multilingualism can be promoted for all children in an increasingly multicultural Europe.

The European discourse on immigrant minorities and integration

In the European public discourse on IM groups, there are two major characteristics (Extra & Verhoeven, 1998): IM groups are often referred to as *foreigners* and as being in need of *integration*. First of all, it is common practice to refer to IM groups in terms of *non-national* residents and to their languages in terms of *non-territorial, non-regional, non-indigenous* or *non-European* languages. This conceptual exclusion rather than inclusion in the European public discourse derives from a restrictive interpretation of the notions of citizenship and nationality. From a historical point of view, such notions are commonly shaped by a constitutional *ius sanguinis* (law of the blood) in terms of which nationality derives from parental origins, in contrast to *ius soli* (law of the soil) in terms of which nationality derives from the country of birth. When European emigrants left their continent in the past and colonised countries abroad, they legitimised their claim to citizenship by spelling out *ius soli* in the constitutions of these countries of settlement. Good examples of this strategy can be found in English-dominant immigration countries like the USA, Canada, Australia and South Africa. In establishing the constitutions of these (sub)continents, no consultation took place with native inhabitants, such as Indians, Inuit, Aboriginals and Zulus respectively. At home, however, Europeans predominantly upheld *ius sanguinis* in their constitutions and/or perceptions of nationality and citizenship, in spite of the growing numbers of newcomers who strive for an equal status as citizens.

A second major characteristic of the European public discourse on IM groups is the focus on *integration*. This notion is both popular and vague, and it may actually refer to a wide spectrum of underlying concepts that vary over space and time. Miles and Thränhardt (1995), Bauböck et al. (1996), and Kruyt and Niessen (1997) are good examples of comparative case studies on the notion of integration in a variety of EU countries that have been faced with increasing immigration since the early 1970s. The extremes of the spectrum are represented by assimilation at the one end and multiculturalism at the other. The concept of assimilation is based on the premise that cultural differences between IM groups and established majority groups should and will disappear over time in a society which is proclaimed to be culturally homogeneous from the point of view of the majority group. At the other end of the spectrum, the concept of multiculturalism is based on the premise that such differences are an asset to a pluralist society, which actually promotes cultural diversity in terms of new resources and opportunities. While the concept of assimilation focuses on unilateral tasks for *newcomers*, the concept of multiculturalism focuses on multilateral tasks for *all* inhabitants in changing societies (Taylor, 1993; Cohn-Bendit & Schmid, 1992). In practice, established majority groups often make strong demands on IM groups for integration in terms of assimilation and are commonly very reluctant to promote or even accept the notion of cultural diversity as a determining characteristic of an increasingly multicultural environment.

It is interesting to compare the underlying assumptions of 'integration' in the European public discourse on IM groups at the national level with the assumptions made at the level of cross-national cooperation and legislation. Across the EU, politicians are eager to stress the importance of a proper balance between the loss and maintenance of 'national' norms and values. A prime concern in the public debate on such norms and values is cultural and linguistic diversity, mainly in terms of the national languages of the EU. National languages are often referred to as core values of cultural identity. It is a paradoxical phenomenon that in the same public discourse IM languages and cultures are commonly conceived as sources of problems and deficits, and as obstacles to integration, while national languages and cultures in an expanding EU are regarded as sources of enrichment and as prerequisites for integration. The public discourse on integration of IM groups in terms of assimilation versus multiculturalism can also be noticed in the domain of education. Due to the growing numbers of IM pupils, schools are faced with the challenge of adapting their curricula to this trend. The curriculum modifications may be inspired by a strong emphasis on learning (in) the language of the majority of society, given its significance for success in school and on the labour market, or by the awareness that the response to emerging multicultural school populations cannot be reduced to monolingual education programming (Gogolin, 1994). In the former case, the focus will be on learning (in) the national language as a second language, in the latter case schools may offer more than one language in the school curriculum.

Immigrant minority groups across Europe

Comparative information on population figures in EU member states can be obtained from the Statistical Office of the EU in Luxembourg (*Eurostat*). For a variety of reasons, reliable demographic information on IM groups in EU countries is difficult to obtain. For some groups or countries, no updated information is available or no such data have ever been collected. Moreover, official statistics only reflect IM groups with legal resident status. Another source of disparity is the different data collection systems being used, ranging from nationwide census data to more or less representative surveys. Most importantly, however, the most widely used criteria for IM status, nationality and/or country of birth, have become less valid over time because of an increasing trend toward naturalisation and births within the countries of residence. In addition, most residents from former colonies already have the nationality of their country of immigration. To illustrate the issues involved, Table 9.1 gives recent statistics of population groups in the Netherlands, based on the birth country criterion (of Person and/or Mother and/or Father – PMF) versus the nationality criterion, as derived from the Dutch Central Bureau of Statistics (CBS).

Groups	BC-PMF (1999)	Nationality (1999)	Absolute difference (1999)
Dutch	13,061,000	15,097,000	2,036,000
Turks	300,000	102,000	198,000
Moroccans	252,000	128,600	123,400
Surinamese	297,000	10,500	286,500
Antilleans	99,000	*	99,000
Italians	33,000	17,600	15,400
(Former) Yugoslavs	63,000	22,300	40,700
Spaniards	30,000	16,800	13,200
Somalians	27,000	8,900	18,100
Chinese	28,000	7,500	20,500
Indonesians	407,000	8,400	398,600
Other groups	1,163,000	339,800	823,200
Total	15,760,000	15,760,000	–

* Antilleans are Dutch nationals

Table 3.1: Population of the Netherlands based on the combined birth country criterion (BC-PMF) versus the nationality criterion on 1 January 1999 (Source: CBS, 2000)

Table 3.1 shows strong criterion effects of birth country versus nationality. All IM groups are in fact strongly under-represented in nationality-based statistics. However, the combined birth country criterion of person/mother/father does not solve the identification problem either. The use of this criterion leads to non-identification in at least the following cases:

• an increasing group of third and further generations (cf. the Indonesian/ Moluccan and Chinese communities in the Netherlands);
• different ethnocultural groups from the same country of origin (cf. Turks versus Kurds from Turkey or Berbers versus Arabs from Morocco);
• the same ethnocultural group from different countries of origin (cf. Chinese from China versus Vietnam);
• ethnocultural groups without territorial status (cf. Roma people).

From the data presented in Table 3.1 it becomes clear that collecting reliable information about the actual number and spread of IM population groups in EU countries is no easy enterprise. In 1982, the Australian Institute of Multicultural Affairs recognised the above-mentioned identification problems for inhabitants of Australia and proposed including questions in their censuses on birth country (of person and parents), ethnic origin (based on self-categorisation in terms of to which ethnic group a person considers him/herself to belong), and home language use in their censuses. As yet, it would seem that little experience has been gained in EU countries with periodical censuses; where such censuses have been held, not a lot has been learned with questions on ethnicity or (home) language use. In Table 3.2 the four criteria mentioned are discussed in terms of their major dis/advantages.

Criterion	Advantages	Disadvantages
Nationality (NAT) (P/M/F)	• objective • relatively easy to establish	• (intergenerational) erosion through naturalisation or double NAT • NAT not always indicative of ethnicity/identity • some (e.g. ex-colonial) groups have NAT of immigration country
Birth country (BC) (P/M/F)	• objective • relatively easy to establish	• intergenerational erosion through births in immigration country • BC not always indicative of ethnicity/identity • invariable/deterministic: does not take account of dynamics in society (in contrast of all other criteria)
Self-categorisation (SC)	• affective (hearts and minds) • emancipatory: SC takes account of person's own conception of ethnicity/ identity	• subjective by definition: also determined by the language/ ethnicity of interviewer and by the spirit of times • multiple SC possible • historically charged, especially by World War II experiences

Home language (HL)	• HL is most significant criterion of ethnicity in communication processes • HL data are prerequisite for government policy in areas such as public information or education	• complex criterion: who speaks what language to whom and when? • language is not always core value of ethnicity/identity • useless in one-person households

(P/M/F = Person/Mother/Father)

Table 3.2: Criteria for the definition and identification of population groups in a multicultural society (Source: Extra & Yağmur, 2004: 31)

Table 3.2 reveals that there is no simple solution to the identification problem. Different criteria may complement and strengthen one another. Complementary or alternative criteria have been suggested and used in countries with a longer immigration history, and, for this reason, with a long-standing history of collecting census data on multicultural population groups. This holds in particular for non-European English-dominant immigration countries like Australia, Canada, South Africa, and the USA. To identify the multicultural composition of their populations, these four countries employ a variety of questions in their periodical censuses. In Table 3.3, an overview of this array of questions is provided.

Questions in the census	Australia 2001	Canada 2001	SA 1996	USA 2000	Coverage
1 Nationality of respondent	+	+	+	+	4
2 Birth country of respondent	+	+	+	+	4
3 Birth country of parents	+	+	–	–	2
4 Ethnicity	–	+	–	+	2
5 Ancestry	+	+	–	+	3
6 Race	–	+	+	+	3
7 Mother tongue	–	+	–	–	1

8	Language used at home	+	+	+	+	4
9	Language used at work	–	+	–	–	1
10	Proficiency in English	+	+	–	+	3
11	Religion	+	+	+	–	3
	Total of dimensions	7	11	5	7	30

Table 3.3: Overview of census questions in four multicultural contexts (Source: Extra & Yağmur, 2004: 67)

Both the type and number of questions are different for each of these countries. Canada has a prime position with the highest number of questions. Only three questions have been asked in all countries, and two of the questions have been asked in only one country. Four different questions have been asked about language. The phrasing of questions also shows interesting differences, both between and within these countries across time (see Clyne, 1991, for a discussion of methodological problems in comparing the answers to differently phrased questions in Australian censuses from a longitudinal perspective).

Questions about ethnicity, ancestry and/or race have proved to be problematic in all of the countries under consideration. In some countries, ancestry and ethnicity have been conceived as equivalent. As far as ethnicity and ancestry have been distinguished in census questions, the former concept related most commonly to present self-categorisation of the respondent and the latter to former generations. The diverse ways in which respondents themselves may interpret both concepts, however, remains a problem that cannot be solved easily.

While an ethnicity question has been asked in recent censuses of two countries (see Table 3.3), all four countries include at least one question on language. Only in Canada has the concept of 'mother tongue' been included. It has been defined for respondents as *language first learnt at home in childhood and still understood*, while Questions 8 and 9 related to the language *most often* used at home/work. The foci of the question presented in Table 3.3 reflect the increasing acceptance of the importance of including language-related census questions for the definition and identification of multicultural populations, in particular the value of the question on home language use (compared to questions on the more opaque concepts of mother tongue and ethnicity). Although the language-related census questions in the four countries differ in their precise formulation and commentary, the outcomes of these questions are generally conceived as cornerstones for educational policies with respect to the teaching of English as a first or second language and the teaching of languages other than English.

This overview suggests that large-scale home language surveys are both feasible and meaningful, and that the interpretation of the resulting database is made easier by multiple questions on home language use. These conclusions become even more pertinent in the context of gathering data on multicultural *school* populations. Given the decreasing significance of nationality and birth country criteria for IM groups in the European context, the combined criteria of self-categorisation and home language use are potentially promising alternatives for obtaining basic information on the increasingly multicultural composition of European nation-states. The added value of home language statistics is that they offer valuable insights into the distribution and vitality of home languages across different population groups and thus raise the awareness of multilingualism. Empirical data on home language use also play a crucial role in the context of education. Such data will not only raise the awareness of multilingualism in multicultural schools; they are in fact indispensable tools for educational policies on the teaching of both the national majority language as a first or second language and the teaching of minority languages. Obviously, a cross-national home language database would offer interesting possibilities for comparative work on these issues.

Immigrant minority languages at home

Given the overwhelming focus on mainstream language acquisition by IM groups, there is much less evidence on the status and use of IM languages across Europe as a result of processes of immigration and minorisation. Here, we present the major outcomes of the Multilingual Cities Project (MCP), carried out as a multiple case study in six major multicultural cities in different EU nation-states. The participating cities cover both Northern and Southern Europe, and Germanic and/or Romance languages are represented. For a full report of the project we refer to Extra and Yağmur (2004). Table 3.4 gives an overview of the resulting database. The total cross-national sample consists of more than 160,000 mainly primary pupils (The Hague was the only city where secondary school data were collected).

City	Total of schools	Total of schools in the survey	Total of pupils in schools	Total of pupils in the survey	Age range of pupils
Brussels	117 *	110 *	11,500	10,300	6–12
Göteborg	170	122	36,100	21,300	6–12
Hamburg	231 public	218 public	54,900	46,000	6–11
	17 catholic	14 catholic			
Lyon	173 **	42 **	60,000	11,650	6–11
Madrid	708 public	133 public	202,000	30,000	5–12
	411 catholic	21 catholic	99,000		
The Hague	142 primary	109 primary	41,170	27,900	4–12
	30 secondary	26 secondary	19,000	13,700	12–17

* Dutch-medium schools only
** *réseau d'education prioritaire* only

Table 3.4: Overview of the MCP database (Source: Extra & Yağmur, 2004: 115)

On the basis of the home language profiles of all major language groups, a cross-linguistic and psuedo-longitudinal comparison was made of the reported multiple dimensions of language proficiency, language choice, language dominance, and language preference. For comparative analyses, these four dimensions have been operationalised as follows:

- language proficiency: the extent to which the home language under consideration is *understood*;
- language choice: the extent to which this language is commonly spoken at home *with the mother*;
- language dominance: the extent to which this home language is spoken *best*;
- language preference: the extent to which this home language is spoken *by preference*.

The operationalisation of the first and second dimensions (language proficiency and language choice) was aimed at a maximal scope for tracing language vitality. Language comprehension in home contexts is generally the least demanding of the four language skills involved, and the mother figure acts generally as the major gatekeeper for intergenerational language transmission (Clyne, 2003). The final aim was the construction of a language vitality index (henceforward LVI), based on the outcomes of the four dimensions presented above. These four dimensions are compared in terms of the mean proportion of pupils per language group that indicated a positive response to the relevant questions. The LVI is, in turn, the mean value of these four proportional scores. This LVI is by definition a value-driven index, in the sense that the *chosen* dimensions (as operationalised in this study) are *equally* weighted.

The outcomes of the local surveys were aggregated in one cross-national Home Language Survey (HLS) database. Two criteria were used to select 20 languages for cross-national analyses: each language was represented by at least three cities, and each city was represented in the cross-national HLS database by at least 30 pupils in the age range of 6–11 years. Our focus on this age range was motivated by comparability considerations: this range is represented in the local HLS databases of all participating cities (see Table 3.4). Romani/Sinte was included in the cross-national analyses because of its special status in our list of 20 languages as a language without territorial status.

In the cross-national and cross-linguistic analyses, three age groups and three generations are distinguished. The age groups consist of children aged 6/7, 8/9, and 10/11 years old. The three generations have been operationalised as follows:

G1: pupil + father + mother born abroad;
G2: pupil born in the country of residence, father *and/or* mother born abroad;
G3: pupil + father + mother born in the country of residence.

On the basis of this categorisation, intergenerational shift can be estimated. In Table 3.5 we present the Language Vitality Indices (LVI) of the combined age groups (6–11 years) per language group in decreasing order.

Nr	Language group	LVI	Nr	Language group	LVI
1	Romani/Sinte	70	11	Polish	56
2	Turkish	68	12	Somali	55
3	Urdu	68	13	Portuguese	54
4	Armenian	63	14	Berber	52
5	Russian	60	15	Kurdish	51

6	Serbian/Croatian/Bosnian	59	16	Spanish	48
7	Albanian	59	17	French	44
8	Vietnamese	58	18	Italian	39
9	Chinese	58	19	English	36
10	Arabic	58	20	German	33

Table 3.5: LVI of combined age groups (6–11 years) per language group in decreasing order (derived from Extra & Yağmur, 2004: 375)

Romani/Sinte was found to have the highest language vitality across age groups, and English and German had the lowest. The near-bottom position of English was explained by the fact that this language has a higher status as a public language than as home language; at home less than 30% of the children reported that they used English to speak with their mothers and fathers. The top position of Romani/Sinte was also observed in earlier and similar research amongst children in the Netherlands, and confirmed by various other studies of this particular language community. One reason why language vitality is a core value for the Roma across Europe is the absence of a 'home' country as an alternative marker of identity – in contrast to almost all other language groups under consideration.

There are strong differences between language groups in the distribution of pupils across different generations. In most language groups, second-generation pupils are best represented and third-generation pupils least. In conformity with expectations, the data show a stronger decrease of language vitality across generations than across age groups. The strongest intergenerational shift between first- and third-generation pupils emerges for Polish, whereas the strongest intergenerational maintenance of language vitality occurs for Romani/Sinte and Turkish.

The local language surveys have delivered a wealth of hidden information on the distribution and vitality of IM languages at home across European cities and nation-states. Apart from Madrid, a latecomer amongst our focal cities in respect of immigration, the proportion of primary school children in whose homes other languages were used next to or instead of the mainstream language ranged between one third and more than a half in the cities covered by the survey. The total number of traced 'other' languages ranged per city between 50 and 90; a few languages were often referred to by the children, and many languages were referred to only a few times. The findings show that making use of more than one language is a way of life for an increasing number of children across Europe. Mainstream and non-mainstream languages should not be conceived of in terms of competition. Rather, the data show that these languages are used as alternatives, dependent on such factors as type of context or interlocutor. The data also make clear that the use of other languages at home does not occur at the cost of competence in the mainstream language. Many children who communicate with their parents in another language are reported to be dominant in the mainstream language.

Amongst the largest 20 languages in the participating cities, 10 languages are of European origin and 10 languages from outside Europe. These findings show that the traditional concept of language diversity in Europe should be reconsidered and extended. The outcomes of the local language surveys also demonstrate the high status of English amongst primary school children across Europe. Its intrusion in the children's homes is apparent from the position of English in the top five of non-national languages referred to by the children in all participating cities. This outcome cannot be explained as an effect of migration and minorisation only. The children's reference to English also derives from the status of English as the international language of power and prestige. English has become the dominant *lingua franca* for cross-national communication across Europe. Moreover, children have access to English through a variety of media, and English is commonly taught in particular grades at primary schools.

In addition, children in all participating cities expressed a desire to learn a variety of languages that are not taught at school. The outcomes of the local language surveys also show that children who took part in instruction in particular languages at school reported higher levels of literacy in these languages than children who did not take part in such instruction. Both the reported reading proficiency and the reported writing proficiency benefited strongly from language instruction. The differences between participants and non-participants in language instruction were significant for both forms of literacy skills and for all the 20 largest language groups. The added value of language instruction for language maintenance and development is clear.

Immigrant minority languages at school

Across Europe, large contrasts can be seen in the status of IM languages at school, depending on particular nation-states, or even particular federal states within nation-states (as in Germany), and depending on particular IM languages, being national languages in other EU countries or not. Most commonly, IM languages are not part of mainstream education. In Great Britain, for example, IM languages are not part of the so-called 'national' curriculum, and they are dealt with in various types of so-called 'complementary' education at out-of-school hours (e.g. Martin et al., 2004).

Here, we present the major outcomes of our comparative study on the teaching of IM languages in the six EU cities and countries of the MCP under discussion. Being aware of cross-national differences in denotation, we will use the concept *community language teaching* (henceforward CLT) when referring to this type of education. Our rationale for the CLT concept rather than the concepts *mother tongue teaching* or *home language instruction* is the inclusion of a broad spectrum of potential target groups. First of all, the status of an IM language as 'native' or home language is subject to change through intergenerational processes of language shift. Moreover, in secondary education, both minority and majority pupils are often *de jure* (although seldom *de facto*) admitted to CLT.

From a historical point of view, most of the countries in the MCP show a similar chronological development in their argumentation in favour of CLT. CLT was generally introduced into primary education with a view to family remigration. This objective was also clearly expressed in *Directive 77/486* of the European Community, on 25 July 1977. The Directive focused on the education of the children of 'migrant workers' with the aim 'principally to facilitate their possible reintegration into the Member-State of origin'. As is clear from this formulation, the Directive excluded all IM children originating from non-EU countries, although these children formed the large part of IM children in European primary schools. At that time, Sweden was not a EU member-state, and CLT policies for IM children in Sweden were not directed towards remigration but modelled according to bilingual education policies for the large minority of Finnish-speaking children in Sweden.

In the 1970s, the 'preparation for returning home' argument for CLT was increasingly abandoned. Demographic developments showed no substantial signs of families remigrating to their source countries; instead, a process of family reunion and minorisation came about in the target countries. This development resulted in a conceptual shift, and CLT became primarily aimed at combating disadvantages. CLT had to bridge the gap between the home and the school environment, and to encourage school achievement in 'regular' subjects. Because such an approach tended to under appreciate ethnocultural dimensions, a number of countries began to emphasise the intrinsic importance of CLT from cultural, legal, and economic perspectives:

- culturally, CLT can contribute to maintaining and advancing a pluralist society;
- legally, CLT can meet the internationally recognised right to language development and language maintenance, in correspondence with the fact that many IM groups consider their own language of key value to their cultural identity;

- economically, CLT can lead to an important pool of profitable knowledge in societies which are increasingly internationally oriented.

CLT parameters	Primary education	Secondary education
1 Target groups	IM children in a broad vs. narrow definition in terms of: • the spectrum of languages taught (Sp < N B F < G Sw) • language use and language proficiency (G N B Sp < Sw F)	• *de iure*: mostly IM pupils; sometimes all pupils (in particular N) • *de facto*: IM pupils in a broad vs. narrow sense (see left) (limited participation, in particular B Sp)
2 Arguments	mostly in terms of a struggle against deficits, rarely in terms of multicultural policy (N B vs. other countries)	mostly in terms of multicultural policy, rarely in terms of deficits (all countries)
3 Objectives	rarely specified in terms of (meta)linguistic and (inter)cultural skills (Sw G Sp vs. N B F)	specified in terms of oral and written skills to be reached at interim and final stages (all countries)
4 Evaluation	mostly informal/subjective through teacher, rarely formal/ objective through measurement and school report figures (Sw G F vs. B N Sp)	formal/objective assessment plus school report figures (Sw G N vs. B F Sp)
5 Minimal enrolment	specified at the level of classes, schools, or municipalities (Sw vs. G B F vs. N Sp)	specified at the level of classes, schools, or municipalities (Sw N vs. other countries)
6 Curricular status	• voluntary and optional • within vs. outside regular school hours (G N Sp vs. S B F) • 1–5 hours per week	• voluntary and optional • within regular school hours • one/more lessons per week (all countries)
7 Funding	• by national, regional or local educational authorities • by consulates/embassies of countries of origin (Sw N vs. B Sp, mixed G F)	• by national, regional or local educational authorities • by consulates/embassies of countries of origin (Sw N F vs. B Sp, mixed G)

8	Teaching materials	• from countries of residence • from countries of origin (Sw G N vs. B F Sp)	• from countries of residence • from countries of origin (Sw N F vs. B Sp)
9	Teacher qualifications	• from countries of residence • from countries of origin (Sw G N vs. B F Sp)	• from countries of residence • from countries of origin (Sw N F vs. B Sp)

SW/G/N/B/F/SP = Sweden/Germany/Netherlands until 2004/Belgium/ France/Spain

Table 3.6: Status of CLT in European primary and secondary education, according to nine parameters in six countries (Source: Extra & Yağmur, 2004: 385)

In Table 3.6 we give a cross-national summary of the outcomes of our comparative study of nine parameters of CLT in primary and secondary education. A comparison of all nine parameters makes clear that CLT has gained a higher status in secondary schools than in primary schools. In primary education, CLT is generally not part of the 'regular' or 'national' curriculum, and, consequently, it tends to become a negotiable entity in a complex and often opaque interplay of forces and agencies, in contrast with other curricular subjects. Another remarkable fact is that, in some countries (particularly France, Belgium, Spain, and some German federal states), CLT is funded by the consulates or embassies of the countries of origin. In these cases, the national government does not interfere in the organisation of CLT, or in the requirements for, and the selection and employment of teachers. A paradoxical consequence of this phenomenon is that the funding of CLT budgets is often safeguarded by the above-mentioned consulates or embassies. National, regional, or local governments often fail to earmark budgets, so that funds meant for CLT may be appropriated for other educational purposes. It should be mentioned that CLT for primary school children in the Netherlands has been completely abolished in the school year 2004/2005, resulting in Dutch-only education in multicultural and multilingual primary schools.

The higher status of CLT in secondary education is largely due to the fact that instruction in one or more languages other than the national standard language is a traditional and regular component of the (optional) school curriculum, whereas primary education is highly determined by a monolingual *habitus* (Gogolin, 1994). *Within* secondary education, however, CLT must compete with 'foreign' languages that have a higher status or a longer tradition.

CLT may be part of a largely centralised or decentralised educational policy. In the Netherlands, national responsibilities and educational funds are gradually being transferred to the municipal level, and even to individual schools. In France, government policy is strongly centrally controlled. Germany has devolved governmental responsibilities chiefly to its federal states, with all their individual differences. Sweden grants extensive autonomy to municipal councils in dealing with educational tasks and funding. In general, comparative cross-national references to experiences with CLT in the various EU member-states are rare (Reich, 1991, 1994; Reid & Reich, 1992; Fase, 1994; Tilmatine, 1997; Broeder & Extra, 1998), or they focus on particular language groups (Tilmatine, 1997; Obdeijn & De Ruiter, 1998).

Dealing with multilingualism at school in the EU context

There is a great need for educational policies in Europe that take new realities of multilingualism into account. Processes of internationalisation and globalisation have brought European nation-states to the world, but they have also brought the world to European nation-states. This two-way pattern of change has led to both convergence and divergence of multilingualism across Europe. On the one hand, English is on the rise as the *lingua franca* for international communication across the borders of European nation-states at the cost of all other national languages of Europe, including French. In spite of many objections against the hegemony of English (Phillipson, 2003), this process of convergence will be enhanced by the extension of the EU in an eastward direction. Within the borders of European nation-states, however, there is an increasing divergence of home languages due to large-scale processes of migration and intergenerational minorisation.

The call for moving away from of the monolingual *habitus* of primary schools across Europe originates not only *bottom-up* from IM parents or organisations, but also *top-down* from supra-national institutions which emphasise the increasing need for European citizens with a transnational and multicultural affinity and identity. Multilingual competencies are considered prerequisites for such an affinity and identity. Both the European Commission and the Council of Europe have published many policy documents in which language diversity is cherished as a key element of the multicultural identity of Europe – now and in the future. This language diversity is considered to be a prerequisite rather than an obstacle for a united European space in which all citizens are equal (but not the same) and enjoy equal rights (Council of Europe, 2000). The maintenance of language diversity and the promotion of language learning and multilingualism are seen as essential elements for the improvement of communication and for the reduction of intercultural misunderstanding.

The European Commission (1995) opted in a so-called *Whitebook* for trilingualism as a policy goal for all European citizens. Apart from the 'mother tongue', each citizen should learn at least two 'community languages'. In fact, the concept of 'mother tongue' referred to the national languages of particular nation-states and ignored the fact that mother tongue and national language do not coincide for many inhabitants of Europe. At the same time, the concept of 'community languages' referred to the national languages of two other EU member-states. In later European Commission documents, reference was made to one foreign language with high international prestige (English was deliberately not referred to) and one so-called 'neighbouring language'. The latter concept related always to neighbouring countries, never to next-door neighbours.

The heads of state and government of all EU member-states called upon the European Commission to take further action to promote multilingualism across Europe, in particular by the learning and teaching of at least two foreign languages from a very young age (Nikolov & Curtain, 2000). The final Action Plan 2004–2006, published by the European Commission (2003) may ultimately lead to an inclusive approach in which IM languages are no longer denied access to Europe's celebration of language diversity. In particular, the plea for the learning of three languages by all EU citizens, the plea for an early start to such learning experiences, and the plea for offering a wide range of languages to choose from, open the door to such an inclusive approach. Although this may sound paradoxical, such an approach can also be advanced by accepting the role of English as *lingua franca* for intercultural communication across Europe. Against this background, the following principles are suggested for the enhancement of multilingualism at the primary school level:

1   In the primary school curriculum, three languages are introduced for all children:

- the standard language of the particular nation-state as a major school subject and the major language of communication for the teaching of other school subjects;

- English as *lingua franca* for international communication;

- an additional third language chosen from a variable and varied set of priority languages at the national, regional, and local level of any society.

2   The teaching of all these languages is part of the regular school curriculum and subject to educational inspection.

3   Regular primary school reports contain information on the children's proficiency in each of these languages.

4   National working programmes are established for the priority languages referred to under (1) in order to develop curricula, teaching methods, and teacher training programmes.

5   Part of these priority languages may be taught at specialised language schools.

This set of principles is aimed at reconciling *bottom-up* and *top-down* pleas in Europe for multilingualism, and is inspired by large-scale and enduring experiences with the learning and teaching of English (as L1 or L2) and one *Language Other Than English* (LOTE) for all children in Victoria State, Australia (see Extra & Yağmur, 2004: 99–105). When each of the above-mentioned languages should be introduced in the curriculum and whether or when they should be subject or medium of instruction, has to be spelled out according to particular national, regional, or local demands. Derived from an overarching conceptual and longitudinal framework, priority languages could be specified in terms of both regional and immigrant minority languages for the development of curricula, teaching methods, and teacher training programmes. Moreover, the increasing internationalisation of pupil populations in European schools requires that a language policy be introduced for *all* school children in which the traditional dichotomy between foreign language instruction for indigenous majority pupils and home language instruction for IM pupils is put aside. Given the experiences abroad (e.g. the Victorian School of Languages in Australia), language teaching programmes can be organised in the form of expertise centres where a variety of languages are taught, if the student numbers are low and/or spread over many schools. In line with the proposed principles for primary schooling, similar ideas could be worked out for secondary schools where learning more than one language is already an established curricular practice. The above-mentioned principles would recognise multilingualism in an increasingly multicultural environment as an asset for all children and for society at large. The European Union, the Council of Europe, and UNESCO could function as leading transnational agencies in promoting such concepts. The UNESCO *Universal Declaration of Cultural Diversity* (last update 2002) is highly in line with the views expressed here, in particular in its plea to encourage linguistic diversity, to respect the mother tongue at all levels of education, and to foster the learning of several languages from the youngest age.

References

Bauböck, R., Heller, A. and Zolberg, A. (eds) (1996) *The Challenge of Diversity. Integration and Pluralism in Societies of Immigration*. Vienna: Avebury.

Broeder, P. and Extra, G. (1998) *Language, Ethnicity and Education: case studies on immigrant minority groups and immigrant minority languages*. Clevedon: Multilingual Matters.

CBS (2000) *Allochtonen in Nederland*. Voorburg/Heerlen: CBS.

Clyne, M. (1991) *Community Languages: the Australian experience*. Cambridge: Cambridge University Press.

Clyne, M. (2003) *Dynamics of Language Contact*. Cambridge: Cambridge University Press.

Cohn-Bendit, D. and Schmid, T. (1992) *Heimat Babylon. Das Wagnis der Multi-kulturellen Demokratie*. Hamburg: Hoffmann & Campe.

Council of Europe (2000) *Linguistic Diversity for Democratic Citizenship in Europe. Towards a Framework for Language Education Policies*. (Proceedings, Innsbruck, Austria, May 1999) Strasbourg: Council of Europe.

Directive 77/486 (1977) *Directive 77/486 of the Council of the European Communities on the Schooling of Children of Migrant Workers*. Brussels: CEC.

European Commission (1995) *Whitebook. Teaching and Learning: towards a cognitive society*. Brussels: COM.

European Commission (2003) *Promoting Language Learning and Linguistic Diversity. An Action Plan 2004-2006*. Brussels: COM. Retrieved from http://www.europa.eu.int/comm/education/policies/ lang/languages/actionp-lan_en.html

Extra, G. and Verhoeven, L. (eds) (1998) *Bilingualism and Migration*. Berlin: Mouton De Gruyter.

Extra G. and Yağmur, K. (eds) (2004) *Urban Multilingualism in Europe. Immigrant Minority Languages at Home And School*. Clevedon: Multilingual Matters.

Fase, W. (1994) *Ethnic Divisions in Western European Education*. Münster/New York: Waxmann.

Gogolin, I. (1994) *Der monolinguale Habitus der multilingualen Schule*. Münster/New York: Waxmann.

Kruyt, A. and Niessen, J. (1997) Integration. In H. Vermeulen (ed.) *Immigrant Policy for a Multicultural Society. A Comparative Study of Integration, Language and Religious Policy in Five Western European Countries*. Brussels: Migration Policy Group.

Martin, P., Creese, A., Bhaff, A. and Bhojani, N. (2004) *Complementary Schools and their Communities in Leicester. Final report*. School of Education, University of Leicester.

Miles, R. and Thränhardt, D. (eds) (1995) *Migration and European Integration. The Dynamics of Inclusion and Exclusion*. London: Pinter Publ.

Nikolov, M. and Curtain, H. (eds) (2000) *An Early Start. Young Learners and Modern Languages in Europe and Beyond*. Strasbourg: Council of Europe.

Obdeijn, H. and De Ruiter, J. J. (eds) (1998) *Le Maroc au coeur de l'Europe. L'enseignement de la langue et culture d'origine (ELCO) aux élèves marocains dans cinq pays européens*. Tilburg: Tilburg University Press, Syntax Datura.

Phillipson, R. (2003) *English-only Europe? Challenging Language Policy*. London/New York: Routledge.

Reich, H. (1991) Developments in ethnic minority language teaching within the European Community. In K. Jaspaert and S. Kroon (eds) *Ethnic Minority Languages and Education* 161–74. Amsterdam/Lisse: Swets & Zeitlinger.

Reich, H. (1994) Unterricht der Herkunftssprachen von Migranten in anderen
    europäischen Einwanderungsländern. In A. Dick (ed.) *Muttersprachlicher
    Unterricht. Ein Baustein für die Erziehung zur Mehrsprachigkeit* 31–46.
    Wiesbaden: Hessisches Kultusministerium.
Reid, E. and Reich, H. (1992) *Breaking the Boundaries. Migrant Workers'
    Children in the EC*. Clevedon: Multilingual Matters.
Taylor, C. (1993) *Multikulturalismus und die Politik der Anerkannung*.
    Frankfurt: Fischer.
Tilmatine, M. (ed.) (1997) *Enseignment des langues d'origine et immigration
    nord-africaine en Europe: langue maternelle ou langue d'état?* Paris:
    INALCO/CEDREA-CRB.
UNESCO (2002) *Universal Declaration of Cultural Diversity*. Paris. Retrieved
    from http://www.unesco.org/culture/pluralism/diversity

4 Prospects for linguistic diversity in Europe and beyond: views from a small island [1]

Julia Sallabank

Abstract

It is now generally accepted among linguists that there are benefits to bilingualism, both social and cognitive. Recent research indicates that it correlates with higher general educational achievement, but only if both languages are afforded equal (or at least respected) status. In addition, the ability to acknowledge and understand other ways of viewing the world is increasingly important in the current political climate.

This paper maintains that strengthening minority linguistic rights will not only maintain linguistic diversity, but also promote bi- and multilingualism more effectively than traditional foreign language teaching. Minority languages cannot be safeguarded using functional/instrumental arguments alone. The benefits of bilingualism can also be conferred using 'more economically useful' languages, although tuition may not be effective without taking into account affective factors. Maintaining regional identity is often seen as increasingly important in the era of globalisation, with local languages a key element.

The consequences of loss of societal bilingualism in a small speech community in Guernsey, Channel Islands, can be seen as a microcosm of diminishing linguistic diversity in larger communities. It may be no coincidence that anglicisation is further advanced in Guernsey than in most other European countries, given its neglect of its linguistic heritage.

Introduction

This paper considers the advantages of promoting linguistic diversity, using the framework proposed by Ruíz (1988) to view linguistic diversity as a resource rather than as a problem. It discusses wider research findings on bilingual education in the light of a study of the sociolinguistic situation in Guernsey,

Channel Islands, where loss of the indigenous language and rapid anglicisation may be seen as a forerunner, microcosm and warning of consequences of the loss of linguistic diversity in larger communities.

Linguistic diversity in Europe

Europe is the least linguistically diverse continent in the world, with only 3% of the world's languages, fewer than some individual countries such as Indonesia (Linguapax, 2003). There is a long history of suppression of linguistic diversity in Europe. According to a legend I was told when living in Brittany, when the Celts invaded they killed all the men and cut the women's tongues out to prevent them from passing their language and culture to their children. In the UK, attempts to suppress Scottish Gaelic were made by the English government from the thirteenth century until the 1960s (Dorian, 1981).

Nevertheless, all the countries of the European Union contain linguistic minorities, for example:

Germany: Danish, Frisian, Letzebürgesch (Luxemburgish), Polish, Romani, Sorab and Yiddish, plus Alemannic or Low German which some view as distinct enough from High German to be seen as a separate language.

Greece: Albanian, Bulgarian, Romanian, Romani, Macedonian, Turkish.

Poland: Belorussian, Kashubian, Romani, German, Ukrainian.
            (Source: Linguapax, 2003)

In the UK, Irish, Scots Gaelic, Scots, Ulster Scots, Welsh and Cornish[2] are recognised by the government, and translation facilities are provided for the first five of these in devolved parliaments and assemblies. In addition, many other languages such as Panjabi, Urdu, Hindi, Chinese and Arabic are spoken by significant minorities. The 'Promoting multilingual identities' conference held in London in December 2001 claimed that 300 languages are spoken in London alone.

For France, Ethnologue (Gordon, 2005) lists the following living languages (numbers of speakers are given in brackets where available):[3]

Adyghe, Alemannic [including Alsatian] (1,500,000 speakers), Algerian Spoken Arabic (660,000), Armenian (70,000), Assyrian Neo-Aramaic, Auvergnat (1,315,000), Basque (76,200), Breton (500,000), Caló [Romani] (21,580), Catalan-Valencian-Balear (100,000), Central Atlas Tamazight (150,000), Central Khmer (50,000), Chru, Giáy (100), Corsican (341,000), Dutch (80,000), Esperanto (200 to 2,000), Flemish, Franco-Provençal,

French Sign Language (50,000 to 100,000), Gascon (250,000), German, Greek, Hmong Daw (10,000), Italian, Iu Mien (700), Judeo-Moroccan Arabic, Judeo-Tunisian Arabic, Kabuverdianu (8,000), Kabyle (537,000), Khmu (500), Kirmanjki, Kurdish, Languedocien (5,000), Lao, Laz, Lesser Antillean Creole French (150,000), Letzebürgesch (Luxemburgish), Ligurian, Limousin, Mandjak, Moroccan Spoken Arabic (492,700), Picard, Provençal (250,000), Romani (48,934), Spanish, Tachelhit, Tai Dam (1,000), Tai Dón, Tai Nüa, Tarifit, Tày, Tunisian Spoken Arabic (212,900), Turkish (135,000), Vietnamese (10,000), Western Cham (1,000), Western Farsi (40,000), Western Yiddish, Wolof (34,500), Yeniche.

A report written for the French Ministry of Education, Research and Technology by Cerquiglini (1999) identified 25 languages in mainland France that would qualify for recognition under the government's proposed ratification of the European Charter for Regional or Minority Languages. Nevertheless, a later report to the Ministry of the Interior into juvenile deliquency (Bénisti, 2004) demonstrates that negative attitudes towards minority languages, both indigenous and more recently arrived, are still strongly established in France. The report claimed that speaking minority languages is a key factor in juvenile delinquency, and aroused the ire of both minority rights groups and sociolinguists. Its use of the term *patois* to refer to both indigenous regional and immigrant languages (whether or not related to French) echoes the report of the Abbé Gregoire (1790) which surveyed regional languages with the aim of eradicating them (see Grillo, 1989).

There is a common view in Britain that the European Union (EU) is monolithic and anti-diversity. However, the EU places overt value on linguistic diversity, as is shown by policies and initiatives such as:

- the Council of Europe,
- the commitment to multilingualism in the European Parliament,
- the European Bureau for Lesser-used Languages,
- the Euromosaic study of minority-language situations in 1996,
- the European Charter for Regional or Minority Languages (ECRML),
- the European Year of Languages, 2001.

This is of course good news for linguistic diversity. And it has had some positive effects, such as delayed accession of some countries to the EU due to lack of attention to minority rights. The Report to the European Commission on the accession of Turkey noted that although the ban on the use of Kurdish and other languages had been lifted and broadcasting in them was now permitted, 'The measures adopted in the area of cultural rights represent only a starting point. There are still considerable restrictions, particularly in the area of broad-casting and education in minority languages.' (Commission of the European Communities, 2004). The situation of minorities in the Czech Republic was similarly scrutinised and found to have 'developed a largely satisfactory legal framework for the protection of national minorities during the last ten years preparing for accession to the European Union' and that notable progress had been found in inspections in 1999 and 2003 (Zwilling, 2004). It is undeniable that EU pressure has led to significant improvements for linguistic and cultural minorities in both these countries, although in the Czech Republic 'Roma still suffer from discrimination in all fields of everyday life' (Zwilling, 2004).

However, in practice top-down initiatives are not always as effective as intended, and, as noted above, Europe is the least linguistically diverse con-tinent in the world (Linguapax, 2003). The European Charter for Regional or Minority Languages is implemented with varying degrees of enthusiasm in different countries: member states are allowed to choose which sections they implement, and varieties which can be seen as dialects of the national language are not covered. For example, Italy recognises languages spoken within its borders which are also national languages in other countries (for example, Albanian varieties in the south, German in South Tyrol) but not the many varieties related to standard Florentine Italian such as Ligurian or Neapolitan. Kronenthal (2003) observes that many minority-language speakers are unaware of the support available from the EU, with the result that very few European minority languages are no longer considered endangered, and the prestige of most continues to fall (with a few exceptions, notably Welsh).

EU policies to promote linguistic diversity do not apply to non-indigenous languages, although the distinction is essentially a false one, based arbitrarily on date of arrival and covert racism. Due to the amount of migration within and in and out of Europe throughout history, very few European languages started off in their current majority areas: English is a mixture of Anglo-Saxon from Germany, Norse from Scandinavia and Norman from France; French is based on Latin from Italy with contributions from Frankish, a Germanic variety, and so on.

Moreover, attitudes towards indigenous and non-indigenous languages often follow similar patterns. The most complete definition of a minority lan-guage is provided by Simpson (1981: 235):

a) A minority language is not the language of all areas of activity indulged in by its speakers: e.g. it may be excluded from administration or education, being confined to the home, religious life, or literature.

b) It may live in the shadow of another language which is culturally dominant because of political, social or religious factors.

c) It may be at risk from opponents dedicated to its extirpation (these may even include native speakers).

d) It may lack areas of vocabulary found in other languages that cover the same general culture. The vocabulary may be influenced by that of the dominant culture to the extent of accepting borrowings where native terms exist.

e) Bilingualism is a characteristic of its speakers.

f) There may be no recognised norm for communication in the minority language, i.e. no 'standard language'.

g) Because of (d) and (f), there may be a reluctance on the part of native speakers to speak the language to learners or even to those from different dialect areas; the language thus becomes the marker of an increasingly smaller in-group.

h) Opponents of the minority language may gleefully exaggerate deficiencies of vocabulary, the absence of a recognised norm, and reluctance to speak the language to outsiders, to demonstrate that the language is 'inferior'.

i) The case of minority language groups may be taken up by proponents (groups or individuals) who are not native speakers; sometimes these may be of doubtful rationality and/or have extremist tendencies – in both cases this leads to unhelpful publicity in the majority-language media.

j) Problems arise in education: what is the official attitude towards the minority language? Should it be ignored or actively suppressed? Should it be taught as a subject? Should it be the medium of instruction for some subjects or even for all?

k) Historical factors may be relevant: the language may not always have been a minority language and therefore may have possessed at least written norms that it lacks now. Hence a modern writer may incorporate usages no longer found in any spoken variety (although this is not confined to minority languages).

Simpson is referring mainly to indigenous minority languages, but similar attitudes can be found towards minority languages spoken by more recent immigrants. Edwards (2000: 216–21) describes the following characteristics of community languages in the UK:

- Uncertainty among speakers as to the categorisation and even name of their language.
- Language shift within three generations.
- Religious institutions fulfil an important welfare and cultural role.

- Not all varieties have a long written tradition or set orthography; on the other hand, they may have high prestige in other contexts, either historically or geographically.
- Smaller varieties of larger languages tend to be invisible.
- Sources of funding for teaching minority languages are scarce, with minimal support from education authorities.
- Availability of suitably trained language teachers is a recurrent problem.
- There is a shortage of teaching materials.
- EU directives such as the 1976 draft Directive of the Council of Europe have acted as a catalyst to develop minority language teaching, but have been resisted by national governments such as Britain.
- Bilingualism 'by less powerful members of society' (ibid: 220) is undervalued or overlooked.
- Standard European languages are viewed more favourably than, for example, Indian languages.
- Many universities do not recognise qualifications in community languages.

Most of these are also true of Guernsey Norman French, which the next part of this paper will focus on. It therefore follows that researchers studying both indigenous and endogenous minority languages, as well campaigners on behalf of both, can learn from each other and benefit from collaboration in terms of research methodology, dissemination of findings, common aims, and solidarity. Such solidarity is not always forthcoming, however. It is unfortunate that in Guernsey, for example, speakers of the indigenous minority language express resentment of radio airtime for Portuguese, a more recent arrival whose speaker numbers are approaching those of Guernsey Norman French, but which has even less official recognition.

The loss of societal bilingualism in Guernsey

When I was at school (1960s), it was the perception that Guernsey French was an inferior language, a language of peasants! One was looked down upon as being 'countrified' if one was associated with the language. There seemed to be no comprehension, or if there was, no acceptance, that Norman French was the language of William the Conqueror; that it preceded French; that it is our heritage! As such, I feel strongly that it should not be allowed to disappear. It is even possible that Guernsey Norman French retains a purity that may have been lost in mainland Normandy, and in Jersey because of that island's closer proximity to France, and has therefore been less influenced by Standard French and may be closer to original Norman. (Civil servant, 50s, male)

Guernsey provides a particularly telling example of the consequences of loss of societal bilingualism in a small speech community, which can act as an example and a warning for other European countries.

Guernsey is a small island (9 by 7 by 5 miles) situated in the Gulf of St Malo off Northern France. Although it is six times closer to France than Britain, its political affiliation is to Britain: it is a semi-autonomous dependency of the British Crown, with its own parliament and laws. The Channel Islands were part of Normandy at the time of the Norman Conquest of England in 1066, and older Guernsey people point out that the island was on the winning side at the Battle of Hastings. The Islands received their special status in 1204 when they remained allied to England after the French conquest of mainland Normandy; 2004 was the 800th anniversary of independence, which focused attention on local identity. Guernsey is not a full member of the EU and the indigenous language has therefore not benefited from EU support for minority languages; for example, it not ratified the ECRML, and Guernsey Norman French has no official recognition.

Language shift in Guernsey is further advanced than is the case with indigenous minority languages in many European countries, with fewer language revitalisation measures. A colleague who visited Guernsey in July 2004 commented that 'If it hadn't been for the place names, the tourist visitor could easily believe the place is monolingually English'. This is in fact not too far from the truth. According to the 2001 census, which was the first one ever to ask a language question, 14% of the total population of nearly 60,000 (1 in 7) reported having some understanding of Guernsey Norman French, but only 2% speak it fluently.[4] Most of the speakers are elderly, and it is not thought that Guernsey Norman French is being transmitted to children as a first language any longer. There are relatively few second language learners due to lack of facilities and negative attitudes.

Guernsey Norman French is not a dialect or creole of Standard French (as is commonly thought), but a dialect of Norman, which is a separate branch of the Oïl language group of Northern France; there are numerous lexical, phonological, and grammatical differences. Over the centuries of diglossia there was some convergence, although nowadays the convergence is more towards English, the current High variety (Jones, 2000, 2002).

Norman French has been spoken in the area for over 1,000 years and was an important international language in the Middle Ages: it was the High variety in Britain following the Norman conquest, and had a huge influence on the development of the English language (Milroy, 1984; Baugh and Cable,

2002). Following the rise of Parisian French in France from the sixteenth century, Standard French became the 'High' variety in Guernsey in a classic diglossic relationship in the terms of Ferguson (1959: 435)[5] until the early twentieth century: i.e. it was used for religion, education, government. Perhaps surprisingly given Guernsey's political affiliation, English only began to make inroads in the eighteenth century, first ousting Standard French from its High domains and then entering the home increasingly in the nineteenth and twentieth centuries due to increased immigration, intermarriage, and the growth of mass media. By the early twentieth century a high proportion of the population was trilingual in Guernsey Norman French, Standard French, and English, but English, previously the 'language of commerce' (Métivier, 1866), gained rapidly in status. In the Second World War half of the population, including most of the children, was evacuated to the UK just before the Germans invaded in 1940, which led to a break in intergenerational transmission and a further boost to the status of English, with Guernsey Norman French increasingly seen as an old-fashioned peasant *patois*.

The term 'Guernsey Norman French' accurately describes the variety's linguistic genus and was used in the 2001 census for this reason to avoid any confusion, but it is not in general use and the variety has no official name. The majority of native speakers I have questioned prefer to call it 'Guernesiais', so that is the term that this paper will use from now on. This is also the name used by Tomlinson (1981), De Garis (1982), and Jones (2002).

There are a number of Guernsey French expressions used in the English of the island, although people are not always aware of their origin (for example, *colimoshow* ['snail', and by extension 'a car towing a caravan']; *buncho* ['somersault'] = English *bump* + Guernesiais *tchou* ['bum'].) Many expressions in the local variety of English are also direct translations from Guernesiais, e.g. 'you get it to Woolworth'. 'Guernsey English', based partly on interlanguage and partly on influences from settlers' dialects (Ramisch, 1989; Barbé, 1995; Jones, 2002) is now at least as stigmatised as Guernsey Norman French and is also the butt of jokes, although respondents with greater language awareness recognise it as another part of island heritage.

Minority and majority languages in school

Introducing an endangered language into school is a common aim of language revitalisation campaigners. Whether schools can be an effective forum for language revitalisation is a separate debate which will not be entered into here; the focus of this paper is the benefits of multilingualism. There can be no doubt that schools often play a major role in reinforcing the low status of minority languages, which is why endangered language revitalisation movements often focus attention on reversing this by *promoting* their languages through the school system.

Since September 2003 a project to teach Guernesiais has been running in three infant schools, with volunteers teaching optional extra-curricular classes of 6–7-year-olds once a week. The scheme operates without official funding or pre-prepared materials. The classes are very popular, especially with parents of British origin, who value the unique link to island heritage. Without official support, the scheme may become a victim of its own success: more schools want to take part and the organisers face the dilemma of whether to continue with the current children, or introduce a new set in the new academic year; there are not enough resources for both. The teachers are all either retired or have other jobs: for example, one takes a late lunch-hour to teach then goes back to work. In comparison, in the neighbouring island of Jersey, the government funds a full-time language support officer and teacher trainer, which has allowed Jersey Norman French to be offered in all primary schools (Jones, 2005).

Guernesiais has traditionally had low status. It is seen as a 'non-language' and can be the butt of jokes. Standard French is still often called 'good French', as the local variety was seen as corrupt French. This attitude is, however, changing:

> The language was derived from the old Norman French, a language of its own and cannot be a corruption of 'good' French, a more modern language.
> (Retired accountant, female)

I have not interviewed any of the 6–7-year-olds learning Guernesiais directly, as previous research (e.g. Nikolov, 1999) indicates that young children's motivation for language learning tends to be based on the enjoyment they get from the activities rather than on attachment to heritage or instrumental motivation. However, I have discussed language issues with young people aged 11–18 from several schools:

September 2001: Year 7 (age 11–12), one class, during French Studies lesson; French teacher present.

September 2001: Sixth formers (age 16–17), 18 students, optional session with credit; no teacher present.

September 2001: one 17-year-old girl; parents present.

March 2002: Year 8 (age 13–14), two classes (approximately 60 children) during Citizenship lesson; class teacher present.

November 2002: Year 9 (age 15–16), five students; supply teacher present.

Although over half of the 11-year-olds had an English parent, nearly half had heard Guernsey French, and a third had relatives who spoke it. They professed not to understand it except 'some bits', but knew what their older relatives were saying when they swore in Guernsey French. Some said they would like to speak it with their grandparents. Most of the 11-year-olds thought it would be a good idea to learn Guernesiais in schools ('it's like – we live in Guernsey and – like – we should learn'), although with the 13- to 17-year-olds the proportion dropped to a small minority. The 15–16-year-olds expressed the least interest in Guernesiais – only one had even heard of it.[6]

However, the 17-year-old interviewed individually, who according to her parents had never spoken about language issues before, stated (unprompted): '[children] should be forced to speak it in primary school'. She also commented 'it would be quality to have our own language'. This sentiment was echoed independently by some of the Year 8 pupils: 'A secret language of your own – cool'. This indicates a different type of affective interest in language, which language revitalisation campaigners might do well to note, as teenagers have little interest in typical language promotion events, which usually celebrate traditional culture and thus reinforce the old-fashioned reputation of the traditional language.

Many people I have interviewed, especially anglophones, suggest it would be 'more useful' to teach Standard French than Guernesiais. Among the comments I have received are the following:

> I think it would be more useful to teach good French. (Catholic priest, mid-60s)

> I think it would be more useful to teach a modern European language such as French or German. (Dentist, male, early 40s)

> If children are going to learn another language at school they should learn proper French or German or Spanish, or even an Eastern language – a language that's widely used. (Retired teacher, female, early 70s)

Standard French is in fact already taught as a school subject in Guernsey from age 9, and it might be thought logical that the proximity of the French mainland would encourage proficiency, but education in Guernsey follows the British system, with many imported British teachers (there is no higher education in the Channel Islands), and as is well known, standards of foreign language proficiency following a British-style education are generally low. Very few people in Guernsey now speak standard French with any fluency – except Guernesiais speakers (although not all Guernesiais speakers speak standard French).

There have always been strong links between Guernesiais and standard French, both linguistic and sociolinguistic. The diglossic relationship between them was stable for 400 years; although Guernesiais had low status, its survival was not threatened until the advent of English.

A way forward

A trilingual model, teaching and promoting both Guernsey and Standard French, as well as English, could take advantage of the close relationships in order to increase the prestige of Guernesiais at the same time as improving proficiency and achievement in Standard French. Teaching the local variety would tap into an affective connection: my most recent survey indicates that even nowadays many Guernsey people, including many who do not speak Guernesiais, feel an emotional bond with the indigenous language:

> I would have loved to have learnt (Guernsey) French at school and to have been bilingual as it is such a gift. People always ask me 'do you speak French?' when I tell them I am from Guernsey – I wish I could answer yes! (Civil servant, female, 20s)

> Guernsey French should definitely be taught in schools, I wish I had learnt it. … Everyone I meet in the UK asks if I speak French/Guernsey French and sadly I speak French, not fluently though, and can't speak Guernsey French much at all. (Environmental consultant, female, 20s)

On the linguistic side, many Guernesiais speakers I have interviewed told me they found French very easy to learn when they were at school. One (who later became a French teacher) recounted how she had not admitted to speaking Guernesiais for fear of ridicule, but her French teacher guessed because she was using tenses they had not yet learnt. An anglophone respondent (a retired hospital administrator) also commented 'Girls who spoke patois all did well at French at school certificate'. This contradicts a fear often recounted anecdotally, but seldom heard from respondents in person, that learning Guernesiais might interfere with learning Standard French and cause negative transfer. Indeed, the experience of Jersey, where the local variety of Norman French (Jèrriais) has been taught in extra-curricular classes at primary schools for longer than Guernesiais, indicates the opposite: learning the local minority variety has a positive influence on learning the standard variety, a second-language echo of the findings of Baugh (2000) and an experiment in Italy cited in Blondin et al. (1998), which indicate that minority-variety children do better in the standard language if their own dialect is recognised and valued.

In Louisiana (USA), where a variety of French (Cajun) has been spoken since the eighteenth century by the descendants of French settlers, in the early 1970s the state government decided to introduce French through immersion teaching in an attempt to preserve the local linguistic heritage. However, the variety chosen to be taught in schools was standard academic French. Thirty years on, an evaluation of the programme showed that take-up of French was highest in middle-class, English-speaking areas, and lowest in poorer, Cajun-speaking areas (Dubois & Dupuy, 2001). Teaching a High variety alone is therefore not guaranteed to promote a minority variety or benefit its speakers.

A trilingual education model along the lines of that suggested for Guernsey is increasingly popular in mainland Europe, where the EU ideal is for everyone to be able to speak their home language plus two others. An international language (usually English) is taught in addition to a local minority language and the national language. Examples include:

- Basque, Spanish, and English in the Spanish Basque country (Cenoz & Jessner, 2000);
- Catalan, Spanish, and English in Catalonia (Cenoz & Jessner, 2000);
- Letzebürgesch, French, and German in Luxemburg (Baetens Beardsmore, 1993);
- Frisian, Dutch, and English in Frisia, the Netherlands (Ytsma, 2000);
- Romantsch, German, and French in Romantsch areas of Switzerland (Holker, 1990);
- Franco-Provençal, Italian, and French in Northern Italy (Decime, 1994);
- Adyghe, Russian, and English in former Soviet republics in the Caucasus (Bridges, 1995).

In the Basque country (where I have visited schools) the sociolinguistic situation is similar to that in Guernsey, but indigenous language revitalisation is further advanced. Even though the majority of children do not speak Basque in the home, many parents send them to schools where they are taught through Basque, Spanish, and English. In a study of this programme, Sagasta Errasti (2003) found that children who use Basque in more language domains get the best scores in English, which supports my assertion that in Guernsey proficiency in Standard French would also benefit from a trilingual approach.

This model values indigenous minority vernaculars as well as high-status languages, but seldom non-indigenous languages. There is, however, no reason why a community or heritage language could not be used, as it would similarly supply the requisite affective input; it would also increase the linguistic and cultural awareness of the dominant-language population (see below).

Valuing linguistic diversity as a resource involves protecting and strengthening minority linguistic rights. The effect can be not only to maintain linguistic diversity and heritage, but also to promote more widespread multilingualism, including the learning of other languages of wider communication.

Educational and social reasons for promoting multilingualism

The achievement of children from minority-language backgrounds has been of concern to educationalists for decades, as they face obvious disadvantages in 'submersion' situations in mainstream, majority-language classes where little linguistic support is provided. This has often been contrasted with the excellent results seen in middle-class bilingual education contexts such as the French-English immersion programmes in Canada (e.g. Cummins, 1979). Cummins concluded that the differences in achievement were due to lack of development of the first language in submersion situations, as well as socio-economic differences. However, in endangered or heritage language revitalisation contexts the majority language is by now often the students' first language, with a (previously and often residually) low-status second or target language.

Recent research indicates that bilingualism can correlate with higher general educational achievement in both languages and wider benefits, but only if both linguistic varieties are afforded equal (or at least respected) status, as indicated by the following studies:

- A language awareness programme in France studied by Nagy (1996) introduced not only high-status languages such as English but also minority languages spoken by children in the class. These children showed considerable pride when they saw their language as the focus of attention at school. Nagy concluded that the project had improved the confidence of the minority children and had helped children to discuss questions of inter-ethnic differences profitably.
- Mospens (2002) described projects in Hawai'i 'designed to promote heritage languages as resources in realising school success'. The research showed that literacy programs in students' home cultures facilitated the acquisition of academic English. Learning was strengthened through improved feelings of self-worth, and school–community ties were also strengthened.
- Reiterer (2003) investigated the role of minority languages in Austria, and found that although the Slovene-speaking population was previously seen as an underclass, the educational attainment of Slovene

speakers tends to be higher than average – *if* they are educated through Slovene.

- A pilot study of 5,000 children attending community classes in Leicester by Martin et al. (2003) found that keeping up a language such as Gujarati could improve students' general school performance because it gave them a greater understanding and more subtle use of language and communication. The authors concluded that such classes strengthen communities and reinforce the importance of education in the minds of the young.

- It has been suggested that one reason why immersion teaching in Canada works so well is that both languages (English and French) are high-status ones, so the children both respect the second language and do not feel that their home language is threatened with submersion (e.g. Baker, 1993; Johnson & Swain, 1997: 11; Morgan, 1998: 31; Swain, 2000).

- The study by Sagasta Errasti (2003) mentioned above found that children who use Basque in more language domains get the best scores in English.

- A study in Australia by Yelland et al. (1993) found increased word awareness skills in children taught an hour of Italian a week; so even the small amount of exposure in the pilot teaching of Guernesiais may be beneficial.

- 'Two-way' immersion in the United States, where education for both minority and majority children is through the media of both English and a minority language (most commonly Spanish), has been shown to be particularly effective in promoting high academic achievement, first and second language development, and cross-cultural understanding for all students (Skutnabb-Kangas, 1995; Day & Shapson, 1996; Cloud et al., 2000). In this model, all students have the opportunity to be both first language models and second language learners.

Looking at the wider world stage, in the current political climate it is increasingly important to be able to acknowledge and understand other ways of viewing the world. More and more majority-language children share a classroom with children whose mother tongue is different. This provides a ready-made window into other cultures. The UK places considerable emphasis on multicultural education, but it usually focuses on festivals and food – very rarely on the children's languages, yet as noted in Nagy (1996) and Mospens (2002), this can be a big confidence booster for minority children as well as promoting tolerance among majority language speakers.

Wider intercultural tolerance does not necessarily automatically follow from the teaching of other majority languages. In the former Yugoslavia the 'Zagreb project' taught foreign languages to children from the 1970s on (Vilke, 1988: 125). The focus was on Western languages of wider communication: English, French, German, Italian. As well as linguistic abilities, the project aimed to foster cultural awareness and tolerance. It therefore seems ironic that these children, now aged in their 30s and 40s, should get caught up in one of the bloodiest civil wars of recent times. Tolerance might have been better promoted by teaching them about the cultures and languages of their neighbours in the local community.

English currently looks unassailable as the dominant world language, but in 2001 Crystal calculated that the proportion of Internet traffic in English had fallen from 80% to just over 50% in the previous few years; this is confirmed by recent figures from the Global Reach website, which tracks the use of languages on the World Wide Web. Graddol (1997) predicted that the languages of the Indian subcontinent, China, and the Arab world would grow in importance in the next few decades. These happen to be some of the more widespread languages spoken by immigrant communities in the UK. The increasing importance of China in the world economy, and of the Arab world in international relations, should be clear from recent events. As Edwards (2000: 226) notes, 'Bilinguals have the potential to make a very important contribution, both within a multilingual Europe and in an increasingly global economy.

In the US, the Bush administration has recognised the value of languages in international relations. Lo Bianco (2004) reports adverts to American baseball fans encouraging them to 'Support your country. Learn another language', using the official 'Uncle Sam' logo. The Center for Advanced Study of Language was founded in 2003 to 'improve America's competence in foreign affairs', especially the languages of the 'axis of evil' such as Korean and Arabic; for example, a website at www.worldstudy.gov exhorts students 'Uncle Sam needs You to study Korean', and a conference on 'Communicating Effectively in the Arab-Muslim World' was held in June 2004 (Center for Advanced Study of Language, 2003). However, Lo Bianco (2004) argues that the levels of competence required for government purposes are so high that 'few monolingual beginners can be expected to reach them', whereas speakers with even a small amount of passive exposure to the languages in the community, i.e. heritage-language speakers, have an advantage.

The US National Foreign Language Center has also recognised this: its Heritage Language Initiative promotes heritage languages as 'both a cultural treasure and a natural language resource'. The Center also emphasises the role of language in national security, and highlights the discrepancy between intelligence needs and the languages taught in American schools.

> Indeed these 'heritage' languages constitute a valuable element as the US
> increasingly is recognising the importance of fluency in more than one
> language. Even in the face of this recognition, however, heritage languages
> have frequently been overlooked in second language acquisition educational
> programs. ... Heritage language students are a rich resource, providing a
> significant pool of language competence on which schools and government
> language instruction, particularly those less frequently chosen for study by
> American students. (National Foreign Language Center, 2004)

Lo Bianco (op. cit.) draws attention to the contradiction between this encour-
agement of less frequently taught languages and narrow assimilationist policies
on the ground, such as those advocated by the Official English Movement,
which has instigated bans on bilingual education in several states. There is also
a contradiction in Bush's 'No Child Left Behind' policy, which promotes education in English at the expense of minority and heritage languages (although
indigenous languages have gained exemption), indicating a lack of consistency
in policy.

It is not only major foreign languages (even if less commonly taught)
which may prove useful to governments. Even indigenous languages with
no apparent relevance to the outside or modern world can prove useful, for
example the use of Navajo by 'code-talkers' in the Second World War. Indeed,
even Guernesiais bilingualism was valued by the intelligence services in Britain
during the Second World War. It would therefore seem short-sighted to discount
a language when you never know it might be useful in future.

The US administration's security-conscious promotion of heritage languages takes an instrumental view of languages, favouring those which the
administration deems of value to the majority community in the current political
climate. Nevertheless, despite the Navajo example, minority languages cannot
be safeguarded using instrumental arguments alone. The cognitive benefits of
bilingualism can also be conferred using 'more useful' languages; although,
as seen in Guernsey, these may not be taught so effectively without a link to
local heritage.

The British-Irish Council was created as part of the Northern Irish Peace
Process in 1998 'to promote positive, practical relationships among its Members,
which are the British and Irish Governments, the devolved administrations of
Northern Ireland, Scotland and Wales, and Jersey, Guernsey and the Isle of
Man' (British-Irish Council, 2004). The Council places overt value on minority
languages, for a number of reasons: asserting regional identity in the face of
globalisation and anglicisation; economy and tourism; and conflict resolution,
its original *raison d'être*. Several studies see recognition of ethnic identity

factors (including language) as necessary for conflict resolution (Daftary, 2000; Ashmore et al., 2001; Kelman, 2001).

The Council's website states that 'Each BIC member has a rich linguistic inheritance and all members are keen to reap the potential advantages of linguistic diversity by collaborating, sharing best practices, disseminating information and material and learning from each other's experiences in a number of different areas.' Despite this stated commitment, the Guernsey government currently puts virtually no resources into preserving the island's linguistic heritage, although it is now finding that economic links with France can be strengthened through a focus on joint Norman heritage.

Conclusion

The languages in which people are bilingual are often low-status languages. The UK now has a good record of promoting indigenous minority languages such as Welsh and Gaelic after centuries of suppression, but community languages are rarely taught in mainstream schools. These languages are seldom seen as a resource but more often as a problem: for example, in 2003 the then Home Secretary, David Blunkett, suggested that only English should be spoken in the home in order to improve social cohesion and English proficiency; this argument was repeated after the July 2005 bombings in London. However, the opposite is more likely to be the case: if we really want children from minority backgrounds to fulfil their full educational and economic potential, their home languages should be supported; the majority population would also benefit from multilingual and cross-cultural education.

Languages are not simply tools like telephones, to be discarded when a more efficient, politically expedient, or trendier communications tool comes along. There has been so much stress on 'language as communication' in the last 20 years that language educators can easily forget that language use is as much about developing relationships and establishing one's identity as finding the most efficient route for communication. Campaigners for minority languages therefore also emphasise affective factors such as identity; a more secure sense of one's own identity is also a firmer basis for educational success than loss of the former home language.

It is now generally accepted among linguists that there are benefits to bilingualism, both social and cognitive. But once it has been lost, bilingualism is not easily recovered. The maintenance of minority languages is thus crucial for several reasons, all of which link the local with the global:

- benefits to individuals' confidence and academic performance, which in turn benefit society as a whole;

- maintenance of linguistic diversity;
- social benefits: tolerance, social cohesion;
- economic benefits, both local and national;
- national security and conflict avoidance;
- preserving local identity and linguistic heritage.

Many of my respondents express regret that Guernsey is losing its character and heritage. The loss of societal and individual bilingualism has led to a lack of facility in French, a linguistic resource which could have been of considerable use nowadays in business and tourism. Guernsey has missed a number of opportunities through its failure to value the indigenous vernacular and its link with French; it may be no coincidence that anglicisation is further advanced in Guernsey than in most other European countries, which benefit from the EU's stress on the importance of linguistic diversity. The loss of bilingualism in Guernsey can thus serve as a warning for the rest of Europe and beyond.

Notes

1   I am grateful to the Economic and Social Research Council and to Reading University Research Endowment Trust Fund for financial support for this study.

2   Cornish was recognised as the UK's sixth official language in 2002 (BBC, 2005), despite the last native speaker having died in 1777 (Nettle & Romaine, 2000).

3   There are a number of inconsistencies in this seemingly exhaustive list, chiefly the separate listing of numerous varieties of some languages, some of which I have included under one heading for reasons of space (e.g. two varieties of Basque and four varieties of Romani) compared to the subsuming of all the *langues d'oïl* as dialects of French. Cerquiglini (1999) explains the status of these varieties as follows:

   Il en résulte que l'on tiendra pour seuls 'dialectes' au sens de la Charte, et donc exclus, les 'français régionaux', c'est-à-dire l'infini variété des façons de parler cette langue (prononciation, vocabulaire, etc.) en chaque point du territoire. Il en découle également que l'écart n'a cessé de se creuser entre le français et les variétés de la langue d'oïl, que l'on ne saurait considérer aujourd'hui comme des 'dialectes du français'; franc-comtois, wallon, picard, normand, gallo, poitevin-saintongeais, bourguignon-morvandiau, lorrain doivent être retenus parmi les langues régionales de la France; on les qualifiera dès lors de 'langues d'oïl'.

   [As a result, in the sense of the Charter 'Regional Frenches', i.e. the infinite variety of ways of speaking this language (pronunciation, vocabulary etc.) in each part of the territory are held to be merely 'dialects' and thus excluded. It also follows that there is a widening gulf between French and the varieties of the *langue d'oïl*, which cannot be considered nowadays as 'dialects of French'; Franc-comtois, Walloon, Picard, Norman, Gallo, Poitevin-Saintongeais, Burgundy-Morvandiau, Lorrain should be retained among the regional languages of France; from now on they will be referred to as *langues d'oïl.* (my translation)]

The Ethnologue classification lists Norman (a variety of which is the focus of part of this paper) as a dialect of French, although it is included in Cerquiglini's list and, according to Tabouret-Keller (1999), was recognised in 1994 by the French government as a candidate for a bilingual French-regional *langue* class in schools (using the term *langue*, a recognised language, rather then the less prestigious *langage*).

4   The same percentage speak Gaelic in Scotland, but the absolute numbers are of course smaller in Guernsey; in Scotland Gaelic now also enjoys considerably more official support.

5   Ferguson (1959: 435) originally summarised diglossia as:

'a relatively stable language situation in which, in addition to the primary dialects of the language (which may include a standard or regional standards), there is a very divergent, highly codified (often grammatically more complex) superposed variety, the vehicle of a large and respected body of written literature, either of an earlier period or in another speech community, which is learned largely by formal education and is used for most written and formal spoken purposes but is not used by any section of the community for ordinary conversation'.

Fishman (1967) extended this definition to include unrelated languages, so that using this extended definition, the twentieth-century relationship of English and Guernesiais can also be described as diglossic.

6   These were the most uncommunicative teenagers I talked to; they expressed little interest in anything at all. This school was situated in one of the most anglicised parts of the island, although here as elsewhere, Guernesiais house names are appearing. Their supply teacher, fresh from the UK, expressed much more interest and asked me for a translation of her house name.

References

Ashmore, R. D., Jussim, L., Wilder, D. and Heppen, J. (2001) Toward a social identity framework for intergroup conflict. In R. D. Ashmore, L. Jussim and D. Wilder (eds) *Social Identity, Intergroup Conflict, and Conflict Reduction* 213–50. Oxford: Oxford University Press.

Baetens Beardsmore, H. (ed.) (1993) *European Models of Bilingual Education.* Clevedon: Multilingual Matters.

Baker, C. (1993) *Foundations of Bilingual Education and Bilingualism.* Clevedon: Multilingual Matters.

Barbé, P. (1995) Guernsey English: my mother tongue. *Report and transactions of La Société Guernesiaise* XXIII, 1994: 700–23.

Baugh, A. C. and Cable, T. (2002) *A History of the English Language* (Fifth edition) London: Routledge.

Baugh, J. (2002) *Beyond Ebonics.* New York: Oxford University Press.

BBC (2005) Cash boost for Cornish language. BBC News 14 June. Retrieved 5 September 2005 from http://news.bbc.co.uk/1/hi/england/cornwall/4092664. stm

Bénisti, J. A. (2004) Rapport préliminaire de la commission prévention du groupe d'études parlementaire sur la sécurité intérieure sur la prévention de la délinquance. Rapport remis a Dominique de Villepin, Ministre de l'Intérieure de la sécurité intérieure et des libertés locales, October 2004. Retrieved 5 September 2005 from http://mib.ouvaton.org/IMG/pdf/rapport_BENISTI_prevention.pdf

Blondin, C., Candelier, M., Edelenbos, P., Johnstone, R., Kubanek-German, A. and Taeschner, T. (1998) *Foreign Languages in Primary and Pre-School Education*: *a review of recent research within the European Union*. London: Centre for Information on Language Teaching and Research.

Bridges, O. (1995) Trilingual education in the Caucasus: language policies in the New Republic of Adyghe. *Language Culture and Curriculum* 8(2): 141–8.

British-Irish Council (2004) Work of the British-Irish Council: minority and lesser-used languages. Retrieved 24 September 2004 from http://www. britishirishcouncil.org/work/language.asp

Cenoz, J. and Jessner, U. (2000) *English in Europe*: *the acquisition of a third language*. Clevedon: Multilingual Matters.

Center for Advanced Study of Language (2003) Retrieved 9 August 2004 from www.casl.umd.edu

Cerquiglini, B. (1999) Les langues de la France. Rapport au Ministre de l'Education Nationale, de la Recherche et de la Technologie, et à la Ministre de la Culture et de la Communication, April 1999. Retrieved 5 September 2005 from http://www.culture.gouv.fr/culture/dglf/lang-reg/rapport_cerquiglini/langues-france.html#ancre84582

Cloud, N., Genesee, F. and Hamayan, E. (2000) *Dual Language Instruction*: *a handbook for enriched education*. Boston: Heinle & Heinle.

Commission of the European Communities (2004) Recommendation of the European Commission on Turkey's progress towards accession. Brussels, 6 October 2004. Retrieved 29 August 2005 from http://europa.eu.int/comm/enlargement/report_2004/pdf/tr_recommendation_en.pdf

Crystal, D. (2001) *English and the Internet*. Cambridge: Cambridge University Press.

Cummins, J. (1979) Linguistic interdependence and the educational development of bilingual children. *Review of Educational Research* 49(2): 221–51.

Daftary, F. (2000) *Insular Autonomy*: *a framework for conflict settlement? A Comparative Study of Corsica and the Åland Islands*. ECMI Working Paper 9. Flensburg: European Centre for Minority Issues. Retrieved 20 September 2005 from http://www.ecmi.de/download/working_paper_9.pdf

Day, E. M. and Shapson, S. M. (1996) *Studies in Immersion Education*. Clevedon, Avon: Multilingual Matters.

Decime, R. (1994) Un projet de trilinguisme intégré pour les enfants des écoles maternelles de la Vallée d'Ayas. *International Journal of the Sociology of Language* 109: 129–37.

De Garis, M. (1982) *Dictiounnaire Angllais-Guernésiais*. (Second edition) Chichester: Phillimore.

Dorian, N. C. (1981) *Language Death: the life cycle of a Scottish Gaelic dialect*. Philadelphia: University of Pennsylvania Press.

Dubois, S. and Dupuis, B. (2001) The status of French in Louisiana, USA: an assessment after 30 years of revitalization efforts. Paper presented at the American Association for Applied Linguistics conference, St. Louis, Missouri, 24–27 February.

Edwards, V. (2000) Community languages. In G. Price: *Languages in Britain and Ireland* 213–28. (Second edition) Oxford: Blackwell.

Ferguson, C. F. (1959) Diglossia. *Word* 15(2): 325–40.

Fishman, J. A. (1967) Bilingualism with and without diglossia; diglossia with and without bilingualism. *Journal of Social Issues* 23(2): 29–38.

Global Reach (2004) Global internet statistics (by language). Retrieved 22 September 2004 from http://www.global-reach.biz/globstats/index.php3

Gordon, R. G., Jr. (ed.) (2005) *Ethnologue: languages of the world*. (15th edition) Dallas: SIL International. Online version accessed 5 September 2005 from http://www.ethnologue.com/

Graddol, D. (1996) *The Future of English?* London: The British Council.

Grégoire (1790) Rapport sur la nécessité et les moyens d'anéantir les patois et d'universaliser l'usage de la langue française. Retrieved 5 September 2005 from http://www.languefrancaise.net/dossiers/dossiers.php?id_dossier=66

Grillo, R. (1989) *Dominant Languages: language and hierarchy in Britain and France*. Cambridge: Cambridge University Press.

Holker, K. (1990) Peut-on sauver le romanche des Grisons? Développement et avenir du rumantsch grischun. *Revue des Langues Romanes* 94(1): 97–119.

Johnson, R. K., Swain, M., Long, M. H. and Richards, J. (eds) (1997) *Immersion Education: international perspectives*. Cambridge: Cambridge University Press.

Jones, M. C. (2000) The subjunctive in Guernsey Norman French. *Journal of French Language Studies* 10(1): 73–99.

Jones, M. C. (2002) Mette a haut dauve la grippe des anglais: language convergence on the island of Guernsey. In M. C. Jones and E. Esch (eds) *Language Change: the interplay of internal, external and non-linguistic factors* 143–68. Berlin: Mouton de Gruyter.

Jones, M. C. (2005) Creation or preservation? The interplay between identity and language planning on Jersey. Paper presented at the British Association for Applied Linguistics Annual Meeting, Bristol, 15–17 September.

Kelman, H. C. (2001) The role of national identity in conflict resolution: experiences from Israeli-Palestinian problem-solving workshops. In R. D. Ashmore et al. (eds) 187–212.

Kronenthal, M. (2003) EU Minority language support: more than just rheto-
    ric? Paper presented at Mercator International Symposium on Minority
    Languages and Research, Aberystwyth, 8–9 April.
Linguapax (2003) Exercise file: linguistic diversity in the world. Retrieved 1
    December 2003 from http://www.linguapax.org/pdf/FileDiscoveryENG.pdf
Lo Bianco, J. (2004) Uncle Sam and Mr Unz. *English Today* 79, 20(3): 16–22.
Martin, P., Creese, A. and Bhatt, A. (2003) Complementary schools and
    their communities in Leicester. Executive summary of report to ESRC.
    Retrieved 3 January 2005 from http://www.regard.ac.uk/research_findings/
    R000223949/summary.pdf
Métivier, G. (1866) *Fantaisie Guernesiaise: dans le langage du pays, la
    langue de la civilisation, et celle du commerce.* Guernsey: Thomas-Mauger
    Bichard.
Milroy, J. (1984) The history of English in the British Isles. In P. Trudgill (ed.)
    Language in the British Isles 5–31. Cambridge: Cambridge University
    Press.
Morgan, C. (1998) Foreign language learning with a difference. *Language
    Learning Journal* 18: 31–6.
Mospens, C. (2002) Language planning as process: negotiating educational poli-
    cies and practices in Hawai'i. Paper presented as part of a colloquium on
    'Negotiating transformative educational policies and practices in Hawai'i'
    at the American Association of Applied Linguistics annual conference, Salt
    Lake City, 8 April.
Nagy, C. (1996) L'éveil au langage: contribution à une étude de l'activité méta-
    langagière de l'enfant à l'école élémentaire. PhD thesis, Grenoble. (Cited in
    C. Blondin, M. Candelier, P. Edelenbos, R. Johnstone, A. Kubanek-German
    and T. Taeschner, 1998, *Foreign Languages in Primary and Pre-School
    Education: a review of recent research within the European Union.* London:
    Centre for Information on Language Teaching and Research.)
National Foreign Language Center (2004) Heritage Language Initiative.
    Retrieved 22 September 2004 from www.nflc.org
Nettle, D. and Romaine, S. (2000) *Vanishing Voices: the extinction of the
    world's languages.* New York: Oxford University Press.
Nikolov, M. (1999) 'Why do you learn English?' 'Because the teacher is short.'
    A study of Hungarian children's foreign language learning motivation.
    Language Teaching Research 3(1): 33–56.
Ramisch, H. (1989) *The Variation of English in Guernsey, Channel Islands.*
    Frankfurt am Main: Peter Lang.
Reiterer, A. (2003) The Slovene language in Carinthia: symbolic bilingual-
    ism? Paper presented at Mercator International Symposium on Minority
    Languages and Research, Aberystwyth, 8–9 April.
Ruíz, R. (1988) Orientations in language planning. In S. L. McKay and S.-L.
    C. Wong (eds) *Language Diversity: problem or resource?* 3–25. New York:
    Newbury House.

Sagasta Errasti, M. P. (2003) Acquiring writing skills in a third language: the positive effects of bilingualism. *International Journal of Bilingualism* 7(1): 27–42.

Simpson, J. M. Y. (1981) The challenge of minority languages. In E. J. Haugen, D. McClure and D. Thompson (eds) *Minority Languages Today: a selection from the papers read at the first conference on minority languages at Glasgow University 8-3 September 1980* 235–41. Edinburgh: Edinburgh University Press.

Skutnabb-Kangas, T. (ed.) (1995) *Multilingualism for All*. Lisse, Netherlands: Swets & Zeitlinger.

Swain, M. (2000) French immersion research in Canada: recent contributions to SLA and applied linguistics. *Annual Review of Applied Linguistics* 20: 199–212.

Tabouret-Keller, A. (1999) Western Europe. In J. Fishman (ed.) (1999) *Handbook of Language and Ethnic Identity*. Oxford: Oxford University Press.

Tomlinson, H. (1982) Le Guernesiais – étude grammaticale et lexicale du parler normand de l'île de Guernesey. Unpublished PhD thesis, University of Edinburgh.

Vilke, M. (1988) Some psychological aspects of early second language acquisition. *Journal of Multilingual and Multicultural Development* 9(1&2): 115–28.

Yelland, G. W., Pollard, J. and Mercuri, A. (1993) The metalinguistic benefits of limited contact with a second language. *Applied Psycholinguistics* 14(4): 423–44.

Ytsma, J. (2000) Trilingual primary education in Friesland. In J. Cenoz and U. Jessner (eds) *English in Europe: the acquisition of a third language*. Clevedon: Multilingual Matters.

Zwilling, C. (2004) Minority protection and language policy in the Czech Republic. *Noves SL Revista de Sociolinguistica*. Retrieved 29 August 2005 from http://www6.gencat.net/llengcat/noves/hm04tardor/docs/zwilling.pdf

5   Figuring out the Englishisation of Europe

Robert Phillipson

Abstract

There are many challenges in figuring out how language policy is evolving in Europe, and what the implications are for speakers of different languages. Issues of language rights and language policy and planning are of concern to academics in several social science and humanities fields. There is increasing documentation of the impact of English on the EU system and on continental European languages, but there are significant paradoxes in EU language policy. Many factors contribute to paralysis in explicit policy formation. Applied linguists are addressing choice of norms for English, but some of the studies of English as a 'lingua franca' seem less than well founded theoretically and to be based on less than ideal empirical data. There is a need to connect micro-level studies with the realities of linguistic hegemony and hierarchy. There are massive forces behind the current marketing and expansion of English, but significant efforts in the EU are going into the maintenance of linguistic diversity. There are challenges in theory development in analysing English as the contemporary imperial language. The need for conceptual clarity in relation to 'lingua franca' is of immense importance. Suggestions are made for taking the analysis of Englishisation forward.

Introduction: challenges

The major language policy challenges in Europe that need exploring, in theory and practice, are three inter-related topics:

- how to devise and implement proactive language policies to ensure that all languages remain viable, which entails ensuring that English is appropriated in ways that are compatible with a balanced ecology of languages;
- how to clarify and elaborate criteria to promote democratic principles and equality in communication in European institutions and

activities, which implies policies for multilingualism in transnational networks;

- how to strengthen the language rights of speakers of all groups, includ-ing minorities, in education and public and professional domains, for which visionary and realistic policies for multilingualism in education are needed.

These presuppose open constructive dialogue between grassroots constituen-cies, policy-makers, and 'experts' on language matters.

To achieve this in the evolving global and European linguistic market, including ongoing Englishisation in states forming a neo-federal supranational EU, is a tall order, not least because, as a pioneer in the field of language policy and planning (LPP), Joseph Lo Bianco, writes (2002):

> Unhappily for those who have sought to devise a 'science' of LPP there are no protocols for doing or designing LPP that can be induced from practice, abstracted, tested and refined into procedures and then transferred across contexts and applied in diverse settings. (…) What I think is relatively portable, at least from my own experience, are *processes for the formulation of policy*, i.e. collaborative negotiated and discursive arrangements for formulating inter-subjective agreements among parties in contest with each other. (…) the field is too dependent on the descriptive traditions of linguistics from which it derives, and insufficiently in communication with policy analysis sciences, with political science, with sociology and with critical schools of thought.

The complexity of an EU of 25 member states multiplies the hurdles in policy formation and implementation. If applied linguistics is to pursue the target of inter-subjective agreements nationally and in supranational EU affairs, there have to be solid empirical and conceptual foundations on which to build. At present there are plenty of building blocks, but all rather uneven, and there are definitely no standardised products and no master builders. How Englishisation in particular, its forms and functions, might be integrated into LPP is also a largely unmet challenge, even though some charting of it is taking place. The need to get a grip on 'English' is being expressed at national and supranational levels. Discourses range from bland celebrations of linguistic diversity, through far from subtle advocacy of English as the open sesame to all the glories of globalisation, to extreme concern that English is imposing an alien monoculture.

LPP and language rights are being analysed in many specialised fields, in political science (Kymlicka & Patten, 2003; Ives, 2004), cultural history (Wright, 2000), international law (de Varennes, 2000), minority affairs and

education (Skutnabb-Kangas, 2000), economics and multilingual govern-
ance (Grin, 2004). Among scholars in critical theory, Habermas (2001) is
strongly committed to building European political unity, which presupposes
a Europe-wide public sphere, a shared political culture, in which processes of
identification would be fundamentally different at the European and national
levels. Many of us academics probably have a strong European identity, our
individual perceptions being grounded in certain types of network, professional and personal, and in the kinds of cultural and linguistic diversity that
nomadism, cosmopolitanism, and the technologies of globalisation generate.
Unfortunately Habermas devotes little attention to language issues, apart
from endorsing the major symbolic significance of support for all EU official
languages and the emergence of English as the default language, building
on its status in small EU countries as what he refers to as a 'second "first"
language' (ibid.: 19). There is a clear gap for applied linguistics and LPP
to fill here.

How then can sociolinguistically informed applied linguistics and language
pedagogy contribute to ongoing activities (Lo Bianco's processes) and open up
new ones in order to figure out and influence the constellation of languages in
contemporary Europe? One major hurdle is to achieve understanding between
people of different linguistic and cultural backgrounds, since such basic terms
as language and dialect mean different things in each country (Barbour, 2000).
Our cosmologies differ. As a historical starting-point for our quest for the
perfect language policy, it is useful to recall that 'Europe first appears as a Babel
of new languages. Only afterwards was it a mosaic of nations' (Eco, 1997: 18).
Nations and nationalism preceded the consolidation of national languages.
The emergence of a considerable number of states and languages of national
power coincided with several languages serving transnational purposes as Latin
was phased out. It was primarily these languages that were learned as foreign
languages in the twentieth century.

The sovereign power of states and of national languages is currently under
massive pressure. A recent book by a French political scientist that explores
how European integration impacts on sovereignty claims that 'the only genuine
"idiom of Europe" ... is the practice of translation', and suggests that language
policies should be pushed in two directions: by mainstreaming the languages
of recent immigrants (Arabic, Turkish, Urdu ...), and by 'stretching the idea of
"translation" from the merely linguistic to the broader cultural level. This is a
decisive but still enigmatic task ...' (Balibar, 2004: 230). Balibar is articulating
a need for languages to be seen as more than merely instrumental, and for
LPP to include the demographically and culturally significant under-class of
non-citizens speaking marginalised languages.

> European citizenship, within the limits of the currently existing union, is
> not conceived as a recognition of the rights and contributions of *all* the
> communities present upon European soil, but as a postcolonial isolation
> of 'native' and 'non-native' populations ... a true *European apartheid*,
> advancing concurrently with the formal institutions of European citizenship
> and, in the long term, constituting an essential element of the *blockage* of
> European unification as a democratic construction. (Balibar, 2004: 170)

In other words the democratic deficit is not merely the gap between the citizen
in 25 countries and a remote bureaucratic apparatus, but also a profoundly
unjust, and ultimately self-defeating social structure in each country. Political
and social apartheid is reinforced by linguistic apartheid. Within each state this
can only be circumvented by the 'non-natives' yielding to the assimilationist
pressure of the dominant group. At the supranational level, proficiency in
English is increasingly expected, even when this puts many at a disadvantage.
The draft Constitution enshrines neoliberal market forces as well as some
human rights. The Europeanisation process suffers from major legitimatory
deficits at both the national and supranational levels, and consolidates a hierarchy of languages.

In continental Europe, English interacts with local languages, with new
media products, new patterns of cultural and scholarly consumption, new military engagements, and new forms of European integration, all of which bring
new forms of communication into existence. For large numbers of continental
Europeans, a degree of bilingualism is a reality, but we are reminded by Steiner
(1998: xii), that 'translation is formally and pragmatically implicit in every
act of communication, in the emission and reception of each and every mode
of meaning, be it in the widest semiotic sense or in more specifically verbal
exchanges. To understand is to decipher. To hear significance is to translate.'

All of us who operate in several languages know how demanding it is
to square the circle of semantic equivalence between languages. In many
European contexts, English has a comparative advantage, which raises the
issue of justice, as well as exploding the myth of English being universally
appropriate. For Bourdieu (2001), Englishisation is symbolic imperialism and
linguistic hegemony. He accuses speakers of the dominant language (currently
English, and earlier French and German) of behaving as though their symbolic
forms and values are universal. Englishisation is integral to globalisation (see
Phillipson, 2003), reflecting broader processes of Americanisation. The language serves instrumental purposes but also constitutes new hybrid cultures.
The challenge Bourdieu formulates (ibid.) is to answer the question: 'how can
one go along with the use of English without exposing oneself to the risk of

being anglicised in one's mental structures, without being brainwashed by the linguistic routines'?

For applied linguistics to embrace a multilingual habitus requires unifying the constituent elements of LPP in a critical language policy paradigm – since justice and cultural vitality are at stake. How English linguistic routines operate is not merely a matter of choice for the individual language user, since we are all constrained by wider structural and ideological forces. A recent incident in the European Parliament exemplifies this. MEPs have a paramount right to use their own language, and in theory, 20 languages have equal rights. But *Le Monde* reported on 17 February 2004 that three French MEPs tabled a motion on a financial topic not in French but in English: 'We had to shift to English in order to be heard'. Specifically the issue was the words 'standard' (in French = normal) and 'normal'. 'The problem could only be solved by resorting to English.' The French speakers felt constrained to use English. If even speakers of French cannot always use their mother tongue, you can imagine what the pressure is like on the speakers of the other 18 EU languages.

The notion that EU official documents 'mean' the same in countries with different languages and histories, different legal and education systems et al. is a convenient, but untenable fiction. One language size does not fit all. The flippant idea that Eurotexts are thinly disguised French in 19 other languages is not completely off the mark, as there are historical reasons for this, and is confirmed in work in linguistic pragmatics that compares the form and reception of texts in French and Danish (Lundquist and Gabrielsen, 2004). In language policy and practice in EU institutions, matters of form and function, of cultural universe and voice, of language and power are inextricably interwoven. We therefore have to make sure that our analytical efforts can capture this complexity.

Assessing the impact of English

When exploring the functions English is serving in Europe, we need to clarify what 'English' is and whose norms are in force. Is Bourdieu (2001) right to claim that so far as continental Europe is concerned, English is not the language of England but of the American economic and cultural empire? Or House (2003) that English as a *lingua franca* is neither Anglo nor American, nor a restricted language for special purposes, but a hybrid negotiable additional language?

Unfortunately a lot of dubious claims about Englishisation are being made. This is so when the EU spuriously claims that 'half of Europe is multilingual' (see Phillipson, 2003: 8). This EU 'data' misled Graddol (2004) into stating that in Sweden, Denmark, and the Netherlands, nearly 80% of the population claim fluency in English. In fact the self-report survey asked whether informants could 'take part in a conversation in a language other than the mother tongue'. In Denmark at least 20% of the population know no English (Preisler, 1999), and the 2003 OECD study of school achievement (the PISA comparative studies of 40 countries) found that 17% of 15–16-year-old Danes were functionally illiterate. Good data on L2 proficiency is simply non-existent. Chaudenson (2003: 292) regards French L2 proficiency figures as fraudulent: 'demographic linguistics can be like the yeti or the Loch Ness monster, a being I have never found and whose existence remains problematical until proven otherwise'.

Graddol also writes (2004) that 'Swedish, like many smaller European languages, is now positioned more as a local language of solidarity than one for science, university education, or European communication.' This is incorrect. More has been done by Swedish scholars and officialdom than in any other state in Europe to explore whether the national language is threatened by English or not, and to engage in LPP. Sweden's official goals are:

- to maintain Swedish as the primary language for all in Sweden,
- to ensure that Swedish is a 'complete' language and 'correct',
- to respect the rights of speakers of minority languages,
- to promote parallel competence in English and Swedish for elites in universities, business, politics, the media etc., and also ensure that there are some with good competence in other languages,
- to strengthen the infrastructure for language policy, in dialogue with many stake-holders.

The position of the Danish government is similar. Universities are being encouraged to make multilingual language policy goals and means explicit.

There are various types of documentation of ongoing processes of Englishisation:

- There has been a paradigm shift from a concern with loan words (Étiemble, 1964), to books appearing with titles like *L'Europe parlera-t-elle anglais demain?* (Chaudenson, 2001), *Lingua franca communication* (Knapp & Meierkord, 2002), and *Globalization and the future of German* (Gardt & Hüppauf, 2004).
- The increased use of English in EU institutions and practices has been analysed (Phillipson, 2003).
- There are studies of the Englishisation of academia in several countries (Phillipson & Skutnabb-Kangas, 1999: Wilson, 2002, on Ammon, 2001, see Phillipson, 2002), and of the reception of English at all levels of society in Denmark (Preisler, 1999).
- A Danish researcher (Hjarvad, 2003) analyses medialects, the new variants of language and cultural form – computer games, email and

internet interaction, SMSs, television programmes (whether transmitted in the original language or the local one), advertising, etc. – which are creatively adapted from Anglo-American origins in continental Europe. The medialects consolidate the position of English, while excluding other international languages. They also open up for 'linguistic differentiation and innovation', meaning that Englishisation affects the form and content of other languages.

- Surveys in all the Nordic countries of the increasing use of English in scholarship and technology, in higher education, the business world and media, suggest that there are strong risks of domain loss in local languages (Höglin, 2002), leading to less efficiency in thought, expression, and communication as well as lower prestige for the national language (Melander, 2001).

- A study of Nordic medical doctors reading an article either in English or in a translation into Danish, Swedish or Norwegian revealed that doctors reading the text (from the *Journal of Trauma*), whether in a paper version or on a screen, took in more when reading in their mother tongue. Open-ended questions testing comprehension revealed that 25% more information was grasped in L1 (Höglin, 2002: 32).

- Study of the key national journal, *Ekonomisk Tidskrift*, from 1965 the *Swedish Journal of Economics*, and from 1976 the *Scandinavian Journal of Economics* (with Blackwell since 1986), documents a fundamental shift in authorship: 90% Swedish in the 1960s, under 20% since 1990 (and 30+% US authorship) (Sandelin & Ranki, 1997). Related studies show that databases used for 'international' comparisons are biased, since continental Europeans also publish in other languages (Sandelin & Sarafogkou, 2004). The expectation that continental academics publish in English influences topics, paradigms, L1 competence, and careers.

- Researchers tend to read one foreign language, rather than several. Figures for translation show that in Sweden a century ago an approximately equal number of titles were translated from French, German, and English. Now most translation is from English (Melander, 2001).

Although the data is sporadic and uneven, it can shed light on whether the shift to English and Anglo-American norms represents a threat to cultural diversity and linguistic vitality. Few question the need to use English in the modern world. The issue is whether it is learned and used additively. Whereas standardised national languages and imperial languages, even when polycentric, had the weight of states behind them, the expansion of the use of English throughout continental Europe is different in kind, although some of the structural and ideological forces behind English are comparable (see Phillipson, 2003: Chapter 3). Many push and pull factors propel English forward in specific domains, for instance research, the global media, advertising, and youth culture. Englishisation is inextricably linked to globalisation and americanisation (which some see as neo-imperialism or hyperimperialism, or merely empire, Hardt & Negri, 2000) and to Europeanisation.

Language policy paradoxes and complexity

There are many paradoxes in language policy in Europe. The European Union (EU) is fundamentally a Franco-German project, with the French and Germans setting the pace for integration, but the French and German languages are on the defensive both at home and abroad. English is increasingly the dominant language both in EU affairs and in some societal domains in continental European countries. However, the economic and monetary union of Europe has been a US foreign policy goal since 1945, including the spread of English (Rothkopf, 1997), as part of the corporate globalisation grand design (www. newamericancentury.org). Within this:

> Britain's role remains an essentially imperial one: to act as junior partner to US global power; to help organise the global economy to benefit western corporations; and to maximise Britain's (that is British elites') independent political standing in the world and thus remain a 'great power'. (Curtis, 2003)

This directly impacts on the academic world because of 'the corporate takeover of Britain' where business 'stands as a guard dog at the gates of perception.' (Monbiot, 2000: 301). Pilger (2003) charges the likes of ourselves with complicity in western state terrorism, since 'humanities departments – the engine rooms of ideas and criticism – are close to moribund'. Can any of us be certain that our efforts are not contributing to this, in a world where all are told that they are either with 'us' or with 'the terrorists'? A world in which, as Arundhati Roy puts it (www.smh.com.au/articles/2004), 'the doctrine of Free Speech has been substituted by the doctrine of Free if You Agree Speech'.

The second European paradox is that multilingualism may be synonymous with more English (de Swaan, 2001; Chaudenson, 2003). There is a fundamental contradiction between the affirmation in the draft Treaty establishing a Constitution for Europe (October 2004, Article I-3) that the Union shall respect 'its rich cultural and linguistic diversity' and the fact that English is increasingly occupying space that earlier was the prerogative of other national languages. The EU linguistic hierarchy can be seen on the Commission website, where all texts are available in English, most in French, and very little in other languages, except for documents with the force of law in member states. Changes in the management of interpretation and translation after enlargement in 2004 are reinforcing the linguistic hierarchy. The ways in which language policy in the supranational EU institutions is being worked through is a complex issue, requiring book-length treatment (Phillipson, 2003), but EU LPP is politically sensitive (there is 'a conspiracy of silence', Wright, 2000) and there are strong forces behind assigning a special role to English. Romano Prodi stated to a journalist from *Newsweek* (31 May 2004) in answer to the question:

> A unified Europe in which English, as it turns out, is the universal language?
> Prodi: It will be broken English, but it will be English.

Neil Kinnock, Vice-President of the Commission led by Prodi, and known for his monolingualism, became head of the British Council after returning to the UK in 2004. He has switched from furthering European interests (and more English?) to promoting Britain and English.

Many factors account for paralysis in language policy formation:

- different cosmologies in national linguistic cultures;
- confusions of terminology (e.g. *lingua franca*, multilingualism, working language) in discourse (politics, media, business etc.) and in distinct academic disciplines;
- linguistic human rights are a recent development in international law;
- criteria for guiding equitable supranational language policy are under-explored;
- limited dialogue between scholars, interest groups, and policy-makers;
- overall responsibility for language policy in the EU is fragmented (Council of Ministers, separate Directorates General for Education & Culture, Translation, Research ...), and ultimately (inter-) governmental;
- alternatives to market forces and linguistic nationalism (e.g. Esperanto) are unexplored.

In the light of such paradoxes and *laissez faire* paralysis, it is not surprising that there is considerable fluidity in language policy in Europe:

- an unresolved tension between linguistic nationalism (monolingualism) and EU institutional multilingualism;
- competing agendas at the European, state (national), and sub-statal levels;
- an increase in grassroots and elite bilingualism;

- a largely uncritical adoption of Englishisation, the lingua economica/ Americana;
- a rhetoric of language rights, and some national and supranational implementation.

Norms in the analysis of 'English'

Do these fluid norms also apply to the forms of English? Some appear to endorse this:

> How English develops in the world is no business whatever of native speakers in England, the United States, or anywhere else. They have no say in the matter, no right to intervene or pass judgement. They are irrelevant. The very fact that English is an international language means that no nation can have custody over it. (Widdowson, 2003: 43)

However liberal that might sound, we live in a neoliberal world order. The position is disingenuous when the demand for native speaker models globally is a reality (though in many parts of Europe this relates to pedagogical norms and materials, and not to actual teachers), when the power of English in former colonies is greater than ever, and when English is of major importance for the British economy. The British Council recently warned that the UK economy is at risk if it doesn't invest in international education. The UK economy benefits by £11 billion *per annum* directly, and a further £12 billion indirectly, from international education. The goal is 8% annual growth across the sector, and to double the present number of 35,000 research graduates contributing to the UK's knowledge economy by 2020. In addition over 500,000 attend language learning courses each year (www.britishcouncil.org/mediacentre/apr04/vision_2020_press_notice.doc).

It is false to disconnect English from the power and powers behind it:

> English being disembedded from national cultures can never mean that it floats culture-free (… or) is culturally neutral. The point may be simple, but it is often elided; and this elision constitutes a politics of English as a global language which precisely conceals the cultural work which that model of language is in fact performing. (Kayman, 2004: 17)

Kayman also makes the intriguing point that the prophets and proponents of English as a global language can be compared to Europeans occupying other continents which were falsely seen as *terra nullius*. Contemporary linguists who proclaim the neutrality of English treat the language as a cultural *terra nullius* (ibid.: 18).

There is an influential tradition in writings on Global English in this spirit (Crystal, 1997: Brutt-Griffler, 2002, reviewed in Phillipson, 2004), ignoring warnings from LPP pioneers like Einar Haugen that it is a delusion to consider that English can ever be seen as purely instrumental (see Phillipson, 1992: 287). If applied linguists are attempting to determine whether L2 English communication is *sui generis*, they need to specify what sort of genus or species of language it is. This presupposes identifying whether its paradigmatic parentage is Saussure or Dell Hymes, Halliday or Kachru, Bakhtin, Mufwene or Bourdieu. Debates about the 'ownership' of English tend to be less concerned with theories of language, philosophy, or culture, and more with pedagogical issues. Seidlhofer (2004, a magisterial survey) argues convincingly that there is a clash between recognition of world Englishes as being exonormatively governed and the insistence on native speaker norms. Jenkins (2002, 2004) significantly links phonology to ideology, attitudes, and context. But I do not yet see sociolinguistics of this kind engaging with the socially anchored functions that English performs, which discourses, in what domains, with what degree of success, and with what impact on hierarchies of language and the language ecology.

A pioneer study of Englishisation such as House (2003) presents some empirical studies and reflections on the nature of English as a *Lingua Franca* (ELF) in Europe. In the table below I report the characteristics she attributes to ELF, alongside which are my reservations about the analysis.

House 2003 characteristics of ELF	Critique
functional flexibility, openness to integration of forms from other languages	it is false to claim that such traits are specific to ELF
not restricted or for special purposes	how is this claim compatible with there being diglossic 'pockets of expertise'?
negotiable norms	it is *use* of the code rather than the code itself that is negotiable
bereft of collective cultural capital	the global utility of English, often diglossically High, is significant linguistic capital
similar to English diversity in postcolonial countries	here English equals power, and there is no codification of local forms
non-identificational	English connotes cosmopolitanism, and in Germany had positive connotations of liberation from the Nazi past
non-native ownership	a concern of the analyst, not the user

When House argues that English is a language for communication rather than a language for identification, there are echoes of a pioneer in ELT: 'The foreigner is learning English to express ideas rather than emotion; for his (sic) emotional expression he has the mother-tongue. English is a rather unemotional language...'. (West, 1953: x).

The identification/communication pair is tempting, as a way of separating English as a national language from English as an instrument for international communication that is less culturally shaped. However, the distinction is seen by Blommaert (2003: 620) as deriving from a functionalist-referential ideology and an ideological perception that results in uses of language being seen as 'instrumental', and as 'a metapragmatic dichotomisation that allocates specific indexicalities to particular speech varieties. (...) matters are considerably more complex'. Hüllen advocated the binary distinction in a less simplistic way, his initial analysis addressing the social functions of English, the risk of a monoculture, and acknowledging that competence in foreign languages can lead to identification with them (1992: 313–5). In more recent work, Hüllen (2002) considers that to see English as neutral, with 'nothing to do with the cultural identity of speakers', is problematical. He distances himself from the dichotomy, since we are in an age:

> with the United States as a kind of new empire. This makes it difficult to believe in the hypothesis that English as a national language and English as an international language are two separate systems, the latter being equidistant to all other languages and cultures. (Hüllen, 2003: 121)

House (2003) presents three types of empirical ELF data. The first is an analysis of how far textual features of English are carried over into German, thereby corrupting a German way of marshalling and presenting information in written texts. The empirical data show that this was not the case. But I cannot see how the written language of professionals translating texts from English into German, of publications originally written by native speakers, can be considered suitable as ELF data.

The second study involved setting up ELF interactions with four 'international' students, followed up by retrospective interviews, on the basis of which the following conclusions are drawn:

- there are few misunderstandings, and the conversation was characterised by Asian participants' 'single-minded pursuance of ... [their] individual script'.
- Participants 're-present' or 'echo' information, possibly indicating Asian politeness, or an urge to reach consensus.

- Participants are supportive and evince EFL user solidarity, visible in collaborative discourse production. This was truer of Asians than of a German informant, who failed to elicit argumentative talk. It is unclear from the article how much negotiation of meaning took place.

House concludes by hypothesising that 'ELF users' native culture-conditioned ways of interacting are 'alive' in the medium of the English language… ELF appears to be a useful communicative tool', with an active component of strategic competence (op. cit., 570).

The third project dealt with the phenomenon of English being used as a medium of instruction at German universities, with international students otherwise in a German-speaking environment. The limited information provided presents English as a transitional language, for international students needing to become confident enough to study in German, and teachers using English as a 'supranational, auxiliary means of communication' (op. cit., 571). There is no clarification of the forms or functions of English, for instance of whether the German teachers' ELF may have created communication problems for the students, or alternatively whether sensitive ELF users, in the domain of English for specific academic purposes, might be more comprehensible than native speakers.

House calls for a new paradigm, building on a multilingual habitus. She distances herself from any notion of a stable speech community, preferring to think of ELF as a community of practice: 'mutual engagement, a joint negotiated enterprise, and a shared repertoire of negotiable resources' (op. cit., 572). She endorses the desirability of identifying ELF norms that are not identical with native speaker norms but rather show expertise in ELF, this being a hybrid, intercultural language. What would need clarification is whether the paradigm shift she endorses can be achieved by analysis of the three types of data presented. In the first case, the issue is whether German is affected by English, not vice versa. In the second, it is evident that cultural norms decisively influence the ELF forms. In the third, the ELF of German university lecturers is presumably influenced by L1 features of phonology, syntax, lexis, and discourse. This makes a rejection of interlanguage, or even of contrastive factors, less than persuasive. And if the goal in such contexts is to prepare learners for a switch to German, perhaps the more German-affected the ELF is the better? Presumably the variant of English used is English for academic and professional purposes, where the relevant terminology and procedures of a scholarly field must be non-negotiable. These studies contrast with House's earlier work (1996) in cross-cultural pragmatics, in which L1-specific ELF traits are seen as a defining feature of ELF rather than negotiable. If that is the case, the empirical base for ELF must be infinitely varied and rich.

It seems fair to conclude that such ELF research is exploratory and that the links between empiricist activity and theoretical solidity are fragile, even when exploring micro-sociolinguistic questions. As yet, there is only a fragmentary anchoring of ELF in (socio-?) linguistic theory. The focus on consensus, negotiation, and diversity resonates with heteroglossia, Bakhtinian dialogue, and a Gramscian rejection of Saussurian formalism and of detachment from historical, material context. However, the essential thrust, as in Seidlhofer and Jenkins's work, is counter-hegemonic: it is about challenging native speakers norms and control, though probably only with a focus on corpus planning, and potentially on acquisition planning. To link up with status planning requires connecting with analyses of language and power, linguistic hierarchies, and linguicism, where the existing research concentrates on different issues, in particular choice between different languages, and the minorisation of subaltern forms vis-à-vis prestige 'standard' normative forms.

Marketing and resisting English

Hegemony is invariably resisted. While some see the current dominance of English in Germany as a 'self-inflicted tragedy' (Meyer, 2004; Gawlitta & Vilmar, 2002), one that has to be accepted (Ammon, 2004), others are much more optimistic (Gardt & Hüppauf, 2004). One German LPP activist is reaching a wider public through a novel set in the year 2010 in which the central theme is the introduction of English as a co-official language with German (Gawlitta, 2004).

There is also a call for resistance to the advance of English in many Council of Europe recommendations, and in the EU Commission policy document *Promoting Language Learning and Linguistic Diversity: an Action Plan 2004–2006*, of 24 July 2003, which encourages member states to create a 'language-friendly environment'. It also states that 'learning one *lingua franca* alone is not enough (…) English alone is not enough (…) In non-anglophone countries recent trends to provide teaching in English may have unforeseen consequences on the vitality of the national language.' Anxiety about English as an invasive language has passed from the national level (France, Sweden, Denmark) to the supra-national level.

Another symptom of resistance is the evidence of imbalance in LPP costs. Grin (2004) has calculated that the US economy saves $19 billion *per annum* by not needing to spend time and effort in formal schooling on learning foreign languages. To counteract such injustice, some scholars have started elaborating scenarios for a more equitable Europe. Van Parijs has suggested that 'whenever a language is the object of asymmetric bilingualism, the linguistic group whose mother tongue it is must pay half the cost of this learning, in a comprehensive sense that should cover both the explicit cost of language tuition and the huge implicit opportunity cost of having to learn a language rather than devoting one's (children's and own) time to other activities' (2003: 167).

A major effort is needed to counteract the falsity of much of the legitimation of the current pre-eminence of English. There is much self-deception in the marketing of English as the solution to all of Europe's communication problems:

- in political discourse: 'English is the world's *lingua franca*' Lord Renton, House of Lords, 14 October 2002 (since three-quarters of humanity have no command of this language, they are evidently not regarded as needing a *lingua franca*);
- in academic discourse: 'English is the *lingua franca* of the European Union', Abram de Swaan (2001: 174), a political scientist who cannot be unaware that there are many *lingua francas* in the EU; 'the language of the proto-European state', Laitin and Reich (2003: 98), two US political scientists specialising in language policy (for a critique of this 'liberal' position, see Skutnabb-Kangas, 2003);
- in international cultural diplomacy: 'English no longer belongs to the English-speaking nations but to everyone', a recurrent British Council mantra, a claim that conveniently ignores British benefits, political, economic and cultural, when its language also happens to be the language of the only super-power in the contemporary world;
- in applied linguistics: 'The ascendancy of English is merely the outcome of the coincidence of accidental forces', Bob Kaplan of the US (2001: 19), and a prolific writer on LPP.

When the Director of the British Council in Germany (cited in the *Frankfurter Allgemeine Zeitung* of 26 February 2002) declares that English should be the sole official language of the European Union, this smacks of traditional linguistic imperialism and incredible ignorance of how the EU operates.

All the more reason for us to work to create conceptual clarity and ensure that the terms we use are unambiguous. *Lingua franca* is a slippery concept: it is a misleading term for what is often asymmetrical communication between first language and foreign/second language speakers. There also seems to be an underlying assumption that a *lingua franca* is culturally neutral, and detached from dominant global or regional forces and their 'special purposes'. The term derives from the Arabic *lisan alfiranj* referring to the language of the Franks, who were seen as representing the crusaders from all over Europe who were out to recover Jerusalem and wipe Islam off the face of the known earth. There is a depressing historical continuity here, since English is now the *lingua franca* of the modern crusaders with a mission of 'freedom, democracy, and market liberalisation'. The American dog also has a flag-waving British tail: in post-communist countries in the 1990s, English was energetically marketed in tandem with the 'free' market and human rights by the British government.

I would suggest that in whatever specific contexts we meet the term *lingua franca*, we ask whether it might not be more appropriately labelled as a:

lingua economica (the globalisation imperative);

lingua cultura (the specific values and norms of a society, country, group or class, needing exploration in foreign language teaching);

lingua academica (an instrument for international collaboration in higher education);

lingua emotiva (the pull of Hollywood, the global advertising and PR giants, pop culture, and how such grassroots identification with English ties in with top-down promotion of the language);

lingua tyrannosaura (Swales, 1997, the language that gobbles up others, linguistic cannibalism);

lingua bellica (the language of military conquest).

We therefore, in my view, need a term other than English as a *lingua franca* for the English of people for whom it is a second or foreign language. The world in which they operate is one where linguistic neo-imperialism maintains inequalities between speakers of English and other languages, within a framework of exploitative dominance, through penetration, fragmentation, marginalisation, and supremacist ideologies in discourse, much as in earlier linguistic imperialism. These phenomena need to be explored in the information society of corporate globalisation and multiple networks, analysing how power is inequitably created through linguistic hierarchies. We need to debunk myths of 'choice', of English as 'neutral'. In education and English Language Teaching, anglocentricity (the forms of English, hegemonic symbols) and the disconnection from power hierarchies (functions) need to be counteracted. Within this framework, counter-hegemonic discourses can thrive (and it is a truism that *any* language can be used for good or evil purposes), but there remain major political and ethical challenges in seeking to establish language policies that ensure linguistic equality and enable all to exercise their linguistic human rights.

Approaches to Englishisation

Hardt and Negri's influential book on empire sees power in deterritorialised networks (2000: 32–3) and stresses that:

> Language, as it communicates, produces commodities but moreover produces subjectivities, puts them in relation, and orders them. The communications industries integrate the imaginary and the symbolic within the biopolitical fabric, not merely putting them at the service of power but actually integrating them into its very functioning.

Their analysis reveals why it has been so important for the corporate world to dominate not only the media but also education, which is increasingly run to service the economy, and produce consumers rather than critical citizens. English contributes to the imperial production of subjectivities, through communicative networks, creating a synergy that integrates structural and ideological elements in the new world 'order'. The key networks are identifiable, and their language policies can be empirically verified. This 'order' is upheld through English at the global level, and through other languages in pyramidical structures. This symbolic violence is invariably contested but is widely, uncritically internalised.

A recent survey by Rainer Enrique Hamel of 'Language empires, linguistic imperialism, and the future of global languages' concludes as follows in relation to English as the contemporary imperial language:

> Neither the number of speakers, nor the number of countries, nor the density of its population makes the difference. Rather, we have to consider economic power, military strength, the ranking in scientific and technological development, the role in international organizations and the cultural industries of those countries and international corporations that back a given language and are determined to operate through it in order to establish the real power and ranking of a language as international (Pennycook, 1994), global (Crystal, 1997) or imperialist (Phillipson, 1992). Certainly agency is relevant, but we will have to extend our view of agency to include all activities propelled by a given habitus, in Bourdieu's sense, not only planned and conscious action. And second, we need to consider the agency of all those who, from subaltern positions and a second language status, help to strengthen the dominant role of a language which in turn contributes to maintain and increase imperial and imperialist power relations. (...) the forces that maintain control over English are clearly rooted in a small number of sovereign states. (Hamel, 2003: 34)

Applied linguists are in the business of control of language and content. Linguicism, like racism, sexism, and militarism, is not only a question of attitudes or awareness. The exploration of the Englishisation of Europe is still in infancy. The final chapter of my *English-only Europe? Challenging Language Policy* (Phillipson, 2003) contains worst- and best-case scenarios for LPP in Europe, and 45 specific recommendations for what is needed to strengthen national and supranational LPP infrastructure, for EU institutions, language learning and teaching, and research. The final two sentences of the book read:

> If inaction on language policy continues, at the supranational and national levels, we may be heading for an American English-only Europe. Is that really what the citizens and leaders of Europe want?

In my view, users of English, whether as L1 or L2, can and must contribute to the critical analysis of Englishisation and to the maintenance and equality of other languages. We could start by listening to this sample of Iroquois wisdom, adding 'linguistic' before each occurrence of 'peace':

> Peace is not only the opposite of war, it is not only the time between wars. Peace is more. Peace is the law of human life. Peace is when we do right and when there is justice between every human and every nation.

References

Ammon, U. (ed.) (2001) *The Dominance of English as a Language of Science. Effects on other Languages and Language Communities*. Berlin & New York: Mouton de Gruyter.

Ammon, U. (2004) German as an international language of the sciences – recent past and present. In A. Gardt and B. Hüppauf (eds) 157–72.

Balibar, É. (2004) *We, the People of Europe? Reflections on Transnational Citizenship*. Princeton: Princeton University Press.

Barbour, S. (2000) Accents, dialects and languages. National differences in the evaluation of language varieties. *Sociolinguistica* 14: 5–10.

Blommaert, J. (2003) Commentary: a sociolinguistics of globalization. *Journal of Sociolinguistics* 7(4): 607–23.

Bourdieu, P. (2001) *Contre-feux 2. Pour un mouvement social européen*. Paris: Raisons d'agir.

Bourdieu, P., de Swaan, A., Hagege, C., Fumaroli, M. and Wallerstein, I. (2001) Quelles langues pour une Europe démocratique? *Raisons Politiques* 2: 41–64.

Brutt-Griffler, J. (2002) *World English: a study of its development*. Clevedon: Multilingual Matters.

Chaudenson, R. (ed.) (2001) *L'Europe parler-t-elle anglais demain?* Paris: Institut de la Francophonie/ L'Harmattan.

Chaudenson, R. (2003) Geolinguistics, geopolitics, geostrategy: the case for French. In J. Maurais and M. A. Morris, 291–7.

Crystal, D. (1997) *English as a Global Language.* Cambridge: Cambridge University Press.

Curtis, M. (2003) *Web of Deceit: Britain's real role in the world.* London: Vintage.

De Swaan, A. (2001) *Words of the World: the global language system.* Cambridge: Polity Press.

Eco, U. (1997) *The Search for the Perfect Language.* London: Fontana.

Etiemble, R. (1964) *Parlez-vous franglais?* Paris: Gallimard.

Gardt, A. and Hüppauf, B. (eds) (2004) *Globalization and the Future of German.* Berlin: Mouton de Gruyter.

Gawlitta, K. (2004) *Der verkaufte Mund.* Paderborn: IBF Verlag.

Gawlitta, K. and Vilmar, F. (eds) (2002) *'Deutsch nix wichtig?' Engagement für die deutsche Sprache.* Paderborn: IFB Verlag.

Graddol, D. (2004) The future of language. *Science* 303, 27 February: 1329–31.

Grin, F. (2004) On the costs of cultural diversity. In P. van Parijs (ed.) *Cultural Diversity versus Economic Solidarity* 189–202. Bruxelles: de boeck.

Habermas, J. (2001) Why Europe needs a constitution. *New Left Review* 11: 5–26.

Hamel, R. E. (2003) Language empires, linguistic imperialism, and the future of global languages. Unpublished paper, Universidad Autónoma Metropolitana, México.

Hardt, M. and Negri, A. (2000) *Empire.* Cambridge, MA: Harvard University Press.

Hjarvad, S. (2004) The globalization of language. How the media contribute to the spread of English and the emergence of medialects. *Nordicom Information,* Gothenburg 2: 75–97.

Höglin, R. (2002) *Engelska språket som hot och tillgång i Norden.* Copenhagen: Nordiska Ministerrådet.

House, J. (1996) Contrastive discourse analysis and misunderstanding: the case of German and English. In M. Hellinger, and U. Ammon (eds) *Contrastive Sociolinguistics* 45–61. Berlin: Mouton de Gruyter.

House, J. (2003) English as a lingua franca: a threat to multilingualism? *Journal of Sociolinguistics* 7(4): 556–78.

Hüllen, W. (1992) Identifikationssprache und Kommunikationssprache. Über Probleme der Mehrsprachigkeit. *Zeitschrift für germanistische Linguistik* 20(3): 298–317.

Hüllen, W. (2002) A world language is born: English as the national and as *the* world language. In C. Finkbeiner (ed.) *Wholeheartedly English: a life of learning* 21–34. Berlin: Cornelsen.

Hüllen, W. (2003) Global English – desired and dreaded. In R. Ahrens
    (ed.) *Europäische Sprachenpolitik. European language policy* 113–22.
    Heidelberg: Universitätsverlag Winter.
Ives, P. (2004) *Language and Hegemony in Gramsci*. London: Pluto.
Jenkins, J. (2002) *The Phonology of English as an International Language*.
    Oxford: Oxford University Press.
Jenkins, J. (2004) Research in teaching pronunciation and intonation. *Annual
    Review of Applied Linguistics* 24: 109–25.
Kaplan, R. B. (2001) English – the accidental language of science? In U.
    Ammon (ed.) *The Dominance of English as a Language of Science. Effects
    on other languages and language communities* 3–26. Berlin & New York:
    Mouton de Gruyter.
Kayman, M. A. (2004) The state of English as a global language: communicat-
    ing culture. *Textual Practice* 18(1): 1–22.
Knapp, K. and Meierkord, C. (eds) (2002) *Lingua Franca Communication*.
    Frankfurt am Main: Peter Lang.
Kymlicka, W. and Patten, A. (eds) (2003) *Language Rights and Political
    Theory*. Oxford: Oxford University Press.
Laitin, D. and Reich, R. (2003) A liberal democratic approach to language
    justice. In W. Kymlicka and A. Patten (eds) *Language Rights and Political
    Theory* 80–104. Oxford: Oxford University Press.
Lo Bianco, J. (2002) Real world language politics and policy. In S. J. Baker
    (ed.) *Language Policy: lessons from global models* 8–27. Monterey, CA:
    Monterey Institute of International Studies.
Lundquist, L. and Gabrielsen, G. (2004) EU – fortolkningsfællesskab eller
    fortolkningsfællesskaber? In H. Koch and A. L. Kjær (eds) *Europæisk
    retskultur – på dansk* 123–65. Copenhagen: Thomson.
Maurais J. and Morris, M. A. (eds) (2003) *Languages in a Globalising World*.
    Cambridge: Cambridge University Press.
Melander, B. (2001) Swedish, English and the European Union. In S. Boyd
    and L. Huss (eds) *Managing Multilingualism in a European Nation-state.
    Challenges for Sweden* 13–31. Clevedon: Multilingual Matters.
Meyer, H. J. (2004) Global English – a new lingua franca or a new imperial
    culture? In A. Gardt and B. Hüppauf (eds) (2004) *Globalization and the
    Future of German* 65–84. Berlin: Mouton de Gruyter.
Monbiot, G. (2000) *Captive State: the corporate takeover of Britain*. London:
    Macmillan.
Pennycook, A. (1994) *The Cultural Politics of English as an International
    Language*. Harlow: Longman.
Phillipson, R. (1992) *Linguistic Imperialism*. Oxford: Oxford University Press.
Phillipson, R. (2002) Review of Ammon (ed.) 2001. *Journal of Language,
    Identity, and Education* 1(2): 163–9.
Phillipson, R. (2003) *English-only Europe? Challenging Language Policy*.
    London: Routledge.

Phillipson, R. (2004) English in globalization: three approaches. *Journal of Language, Identity and Education* 3(1): 73–84.

Phillipson, R. and Skutnabb-Kangas. T. (1999) Englishisation: one dimension of globalization. *English in a Changing World, AILA Review* 13: 17–36.

Pilger, J. (2003) *The New Rulers of the World*. London: Verso.

Preisler, B. (1999) Functions and forms of English in a European EFL country. In T. Bex and R. J. Watts (eds) *Standard English: the widening debate*, 239–67. London: Routledge.

Sandelin, B. and Ranki, S. (1997) Internationalization or Americanization of Swedish economics? *The European Journal of the History of Economic Thought* 4(2): 284–98.

Sandelin, B. and Sarafogkou, N. (2004) Language and scientific publication statistics. *Language Problems and Language Planning* 28(1): 1–10.

Seidlhofer, B. (2004) Research perspectives on teaching English as a lingua franca. *Annual Review of Applied Linguistics* 24: 209–39.

Skutnabb-Kangas, T. (2000) *Linguistic genocide in education – or worldwide diversity and human rights?* Mahwah, NJ: Lawrence Erlbaum.

Skutnabb-Kangas, T. (2003) Lecture at Glendon College, University of York, Toronto, 14 October. Available on www.glendon.yorku.ca/englishstudies/events.html

Steiner, G. (1998) *After Babel. Aspects of Language and Translation*. Oxford: Oxford University Press.

Swales, J. (1997) English as 'Tyrannosaurus Rex'. *World Englishes* 16(3): 373–82.

Van Parijs, P. (2003) Linguistic justice. In W. Kymlicka and A. Patten (eds) *Language Rights and Political Theory* 153–68. Oxford: Oxford University Press.

West, M. (1953) Introduction. *A General Service List of English Words*. London: Longman.

Widdowson, H. G. (2003) *Defining Issues in English Language Teaching*. Oxford: Oxford University Press.

Wilson, D. (2002) *The Englishisation of Academe: a Finnish perspective*. Jyväskylä: University of Jyväskylä Language Centre.

Wright, S. (2000) *Community and Communication. The Role of Language in Nation State Building and European Integration*. Clevedon: Multilingual Matters.

6   Unity in diversity: English as a lingua franca for Europe

Juliane House

Abstract

In this paper I discuss ways of managing linguistic and cultural diversity in Europe. I argue that the adoption of a lingua franca as a useful communicative tool does not necessarily pose a threat to multilingualism in Europe, rather it may be the only realistic way of coping with a multitude of languages in contact. Paradoxically, the use of a lingua franca may become a means of ensuring and indeed promoting diversity. Having brought forward a number of arguments against making use of English as a lingua franca in Europe, I try to relativise these arguments by pointing to the distinction between 'languages for communication' and 'languages for identification', and by drawing on the findings of several relevant research projects. Finally, I make a few suggestions as to how applied linguistics can contribute to reconfiguring Europe.

Introduction: the nature of English as a lingua franca

In its original meaning, a *lingua franca* – the term comes from Arabic *lisan-al-farang* – was simply an intermediary language used by speakers of Arabic with travellers from Western Europe. Its meaning was later extended to describe a language of commerce, a rather stable variety with little room for individual variation. This meaning is clearly not applicable to today's global English, whose major characteristic is its enormous functional flexibility and spread across many different linguistic areas – two features that have led to the remarkable fact that the number of non-native speakers is now substantially larger than that of its native speakers. ELF is today no longer 'owned' by its native speakers, and there is a strong tendency towards further, more rapid 'de-owning' – a process which leads to an increasing diversification of English through acculturation and nativisation processes.

The fact that English is used today to cover an unprecedented range of domains and functions worldwide is so new in the history of language contacts that new theoretical and descriptive perspectives are needed to adequately handle the phenomenon. In the case of English we are not dealing with one monolithic, 'hegemonic' English voice, but with a great diversity of different localised voices in domains such as business, politics, science, student and touristic encounters, technology and media discourse. True, there are still attempts by the inner circle of native speakers to perpetuate bygone dichotomies of 'us' versus 'them', one way translation avenues, control of access to prestigious organisations and publication organs, and subtle put-downs of non-native speakers of English. However, these have less to do with English as a language; rather, they reflect real world differences in economic, political and professional status and power. The English language today has largely outgrown the one-sided manipulations of the inner circle and has become – not least through the importance of ELF discourse – a powerful tool for national, regional and local renaissance and resistance by its new expert non-native users.

ELF's main characteristic, then, is its multiplicity of voices. When English is used in interactions between, say, German and Spanish speakers, underlying differences in interactional norms, in standards of politeness, directness, values, feelings of cultural and historical tradition remain exactly what they were – these norms are not shared, nor need they be. And it is this deep diversity in the communicative use of English as a *lingua franca* by speakers with different mother tongues and backgrounds, which clearly invalidates the claim that English is a 'killer language'. Which English, one may ask? Is it those localised, regionalised or otherwise appropriated varieties whose linguistic surface is English, but whose speakers creatively conduct pragmatic shifts in their use of ELF? Surely not! Non-native speakers of English – in Europe as anywhere in the world – are fast developing their own discourse strategies, speech act modifications, genres and communicative styles. And they choose to do this out of their own free will. But exactly how does ELF differ from native English? Is ELF a language for specific purposes, a pidgin, a species of 'foreigner talk'? Can it be linked to particular speech events or is it a particular type of interlanguage?

ELF is not a language for specific purposes, and it is not a pidgin, because it is neither a restricted language nor a minimal language, but a language showing full linguistic and functional range – a necessary condition for enabling communication between people who would otherwise not be able to communicate. ELF cannot be equated with 'foreigner talk' – such a concept would be too ideologically loaded because ELF refers to language use from the perspective of an unprejudiced description of a 'contact language between persons who neither share a common native tongue nor a common national culture, and for whom English is the chosen language of communication' (Firth, 1996: 20). In ELF there is 'no consistency in form that goes beyond the participant level, i.e. each group of interactants seems to negotiate its own variety of *lingua franca* use in terms of proficiency level, use of code-mixing, etc.' (Gramkow Andersen, 1993: 108). Here we have ELF's most important ingredients: negotiability, variability in terms of speaker proficiency, openness to an integration of forms of other languages. All this reminds us of an 'interlanguage' (Selinker, 1972) with its salient notions of 'foreign norm', 'error', 'system' and 'the native speaker'. But it is vis-à-vis these notions that the differential approach to ELF can now be outlined. First, ELF speakers cannot be conceived with a view to an ideal native speaker norm, they are not by definition not fully competent in the part of their linguistic knowledge under study. Second, the object of inquiry is not a psycholinguistic 'interim' system developing in a speaker on her path towards full mastery of the English language system, towards becoming a 'proper member' of another speech community. In the interlanguage approach a speaker's L2 English knowledge in her role as a learner, whose competence always differs in some way from that of a native speaker is in focus. ELF on the other hand is to be seen as a multivoiced, multilingual use of English in its own right with knowledge of other languages recognised as genotypical, if not phenotypically present.

More adequate for ELF than the interlanguage frame of reference is thus the multilingual speaker, who possesses more than one set of linguistic and sociocultural knowledge and has 'multicompetence' (Cook, 1993). And the focus is on language **use** rather than on development and acquisition, and on the sociopragmatic functions of language **choice**. Conceptually useful for ELF is also Grosjean's (2001) modelling a bilingual speaker's competence in terms of different language modes being variously activated, such that a bilingual speaker may be in 'the bilingual mode of speech production' when both her languages are simultaneously active.

Another useful conceptualising of ELF comes from Widdowson (2003). He introduces the notion of a 'virtual language', arguing that it is English as a virtual language that is being 'spread' and 'actualised' and subjected to local constraints in the process. Widdowson suggests that ELF is a register, i.e. a variety of use, and in the case of ELF this variety is used by expert communities as exploitations of the resources of virtual English, and as such ELF regulates itself quite independently of native English speakers. While World Englishes are dialect-like serving the immediate communicative needs in a particular, stable community, ELF is secondary and global and associated with particular domains of use. Local 'dialectal' varieties of English are outer circle phenomena, whose speakers are typically speakers of L2 English. Global ELF registers, in which the dynamism of international spread is most noticeable, can be taken up by speakers in both, indeed in all circles, because in ELF all speakers of English – as first, second or foreign language – are in a sense in the same expanding circle.

In sum then, ELF appears to be neither a restricted language for special purposes, nor a pidgin, nor a brand of foreigner talk, nor an interlanguage, but one of a repertoire of different communicative instruments or registers an individual has at her disposal, a useful and versatile tool, in short a 'language for communication'. As such it can be distinguished from those other parts of the individual's repertoire which serve as 'language(s) for identification' (Hüllen, 1992). This distinction is a functional one, and it is in line with a view of language as an instrument which fulfils different functions in human experience. As a language for communication ELF is a useful tool for facilitating communication inside the new Europe of 25 member states and 20 official languages. (House, 2003a). Many arguments have, however, been brought forward against the idea of adopting ELF for Europe. In the following I will present some of these arguments, and in an attempt to refute them I will discuss some relevant empirical research.

The issue of ELF as a 'language of communication' in the EU argued from four perspectives

Sociopolitical perspectives

When speakers use English as 'a language for communication', they are unlikely to conceive of it as a 'language for identification'. It is local languages, an individual's L1(s) that are likely to be the determinants of identity – identity in the sense of holding a stake in the collective linguistic-cultural capital that defines the L1 group and its members. ELF is a transactional language used for speakers' very own communicative purposes and advantages. If one wants to communicate beyond one's own local or regional circle, one will have to (and often want to) use a language with a high 'communication value (Q-value)' (de Swaan, 2001: 33ff) that links one with wider circles of communication. It is often inadvisable to impose concerns of hegemonic English on people in circumstances one cannot fully know, as an e-mail I recently received from a Hongkong colleague reveals:

> I always feel that non-native speakers of English are forever caught in a kind of double bind. Take for example those of us who were brought up in Hong Kong. I got criticized at school and university if I didn't speak English, but I also got criticized (mostly by those who pretended to be politically correct) if I spoke English. It was only in the last few years that I stopped wishing I had two mouths. English, I believe, can never replace our mother tongue, certainly not where the emotional intensity of feelings is concerned.

Using ELF for instrumental purposes does not necessarily displace national or local languages, since they are used for different purposes. As Bisong (1995) points out with reference to Nigeria, English has become one of the languages available for use, and it is its communication potential which makes people decide for English. Arguments such as the ones brought forward by people warning us against the consequences of the spread of ELF may well be patronising in that they imply that ELF users do not know what is in their own interest. Paradoxical as this may seem, the very spread of ELF often stimulates members of minority languages to insist on their own local language for emotional binding to their own culture, history and tradition, and there is, indeed, a strong counter-current to the spread of ELF in that local varieties and cultural practices are often strengthened. One example is the revival of German language folk music, songs in local dialects such as Bavarian to counteract pop music in English only. So using ELF as a medium of border crossing to set up as many expert communities as necessary in science, economics, education etc. cannot only be seen as encroaching on established 'roots'.

Recent examples show that even the Internet thought to be a classic spreader of English is now increasingly appropriated by non-native ELF users. Bloch (2004) has examined how Chinese writers use the Internet to produce a rhetoric that incorporates traditional Chinese rhetorical forms expressed in the medium of the English language. Similarly, Lam (2004) reports on how global practices of English on the Internet intersect with local practices of English in territorial and national spheres, and how the Internet can help articulate new ways of using English. She describes discursive practices in a Chinese/English bilingual chat room and shows how a mixed-code variety of English is deliberately adopted by the bilinguals for constructing them as speakers of both English and Cantonese.

As a variety with a high communicative value, ELF has a special status in the EU that sets it off from all other EU languages. In the absence of any explicit EU language policy, a 'mute immobility in matters of language prepares the ground for a stampede towards English' (de Swaan, 2001: 171). It is also an open secret that the EU's supposedly humane multilingualism is but an illusion in that some EU languages have always been more equal than others: From the outset, French, supported by an aggressive language policy, has held a singularly privileged position as the only official language of the EU's precursor, and as a language spoken in all three major EU domiciles. Since the French privilege is now being threatened, a fierce rivalry between French and English has developed, but English has become the EU's de facto *lingua franca*, although its role has been consistently tabooed. As Watts (2001) has implied in his critique of both the EU's and Switzerland's ideology of multilingualism, planning for multilingualism and deliberately failing to discuss ELF's role in a

'Europe of mother tongues' may point to a subtext. This subtext gives in fact unilateral protection to other European languages, and it gives in to the pressure of lobbyists from professions such as translators, interpreters and the steadily increasing number of people in the intercultural, multicultural, communicative etc. consultancy and advice business.

The illusion of multilingualism in the EU and the lip service paid to the ideal of a multiplicity of languages reflected in Europeans' plurilingualism, is also costly and cumbersome, witness the unwieldy machinery of translation, which might become difficult to uphold once there are more than 30 member states. Based on insider experience, Koskinen (2000) claims that the EU commission's translation bureau, the largest in the world, entertains dangerous 'institutional illusions' translating the EU's illusion of equality into both an illusion of multilingualism and of facile translatability. As 'a service with a mission', the value of translation is that of a living symbol of the high ideal of equality, i.e. it is important that a translation exists, not what it is like and does. Translators sometimes suspect that no one actually reads their finished translations. Important working papers are quickly read in English, once the translations are ready, the new information is old information – due to the simple fact that for a translation to come into being there has to be an original – inherent in a translation is therefore its delayed nature. Many people also doubt the accuracy of the translation and openly prefer to read the more reliable English (and French) originals. Another curious feature of EU translations is that they are often not marked as translations as though the process of translation had no effect on a document – more evidence of the erroneous assumption that translation is an automatic, mechanistic process. In other words, the illusion of linguistic equality perverts the act of translation since it implies that a translation is but a version of 'the same thing' critically dismissing real-life cultural differences that need to be taken account in 'cultural filtering' (House, 1997). Ironically, therefore, despite the EU's ideology of multiculturalism, the ideology of equality prevents cultural adaptations (see Tosi, this volume).

The EU's ostensible multilingualism is one of its key characteristics, which also distinguishes it from other international organisations. Instead of having opted for only two or three working languages, all the official languages of the member states (in the beginning four, now five times four!) were given equal status. This policy was once justified because the EU was to function at an inter-governmental level with its legislation having direct consequences for the lives of ordinary people (i.e. what food they eat and what it costs). For a smoother functioning of the EU's institutions however the use of a *lingua franca* has many advantages. If one accepts the distinction between languages for communication and languages for identification, this need not be a problem. The dangers of globalisation and capitalist expansion, and the McDonaldisation of Europe have extra-linguistic roots and are linked to the economic supremacy of the US. Introducing ELF to the EU might help Europe's political integration by lowering the language barrier and opening the way for a common European stance in world politics – as a counterweight to the US superpower. The strongest opposition to this idea will come from France. The advent of the ten central European countries – most of whom favour English – is threatening to marginalise French in the long run – a tendency reinforced by the fact that increased use of ELF in the EU institutions will also have an impact on the use of English in the ministries of the member states. However, it is surely better to lead an open debate about these issues than to ignore them.

Linguistic perspectives

One of the most frequent linguistic arguments against adopting ELF in Europe relates to the 'unfair disadvantage' ELF speakers have vis-à-vis native English speakers. They are thought to never be able to overcome the handicap of their 'reduced personalities' in the medium of ELF, i.e. will never be as witty, persuasive or creative as they are in their L1s. But how is one to judge the validity of this claim? Anecdotal evidence will not do. Some more reliable evidence now comes from research on how ELF speakers actually behave in ELF communicative situations. I will give one example of such research in what follows.

The Hamburg project 'communicating in English as a lingua franca'

In this project (House, 2002), we are looking at the nature of ELF interactions. Groups of four students from many different L1 backgrounds were asked to interact (following a stimulus in the form of an article on ELF) and to also provide retrospective feedback on these interactions. To validate the analyses, comparable native English and (whenever possible) L1 interactions were also enacted, with subjective metapragmatic assessments substantiating the analysis. One of the most remarkable findings that has emerged from both the interaction analysis and the subjective assessments is that there are very few misunderstandings and a concomitant frequency of 'let it pass' behaviour, both of which make the discourse robust, meaningful and ordinary (cf. Firth, 1996; Lesznyák, 2004, for similar results). The paucity of misunderstandings is in stark contrast to previous analyses of native-non-native talk which revealed many and varied misunderstandings (House, 2003b). In its robustness, ELF talk thus seems to be qualitatively different in nature. This impression is based on three points:

1. Although interactants seem to transfer L1 conventions into their ELF dis-
    course – e.g. Asian interactants recycle a specific topic regardless of where
    and how the discourse has developed at any particular point – this never
    leads to a breakdown of the interaction. In the retrospective interviews,
    a participant suggested that such topic recycling stems from transfer of
    native Indonesian convention of discourse construction.

2. A second finding refers to the remarkably frequent use of a particular dis-
    course marker: the *Represent* (Edmondson, 1981), with which the previous
    speaker's move is 'represented' so as to aid the current speaker's working
    memory in both her comprehension and production processes, to provide
    textual coherence, signal uptake, request confirmation or indicate to the
    previous speaker that one does not intend to 'steal' her turn. *Represents*
    – often used as 'echoing', 'mirroring', or 'shadowing' devices – also occur
    in therapeutic interviews, classroom discourse and aviation control dis-
    course. They act simultaneously as an encapsulation of previously given
    information and as a new instantiation creating linkage across turns through
    redundancy and the construction of lexical paradigmatic clusters. But
    Represents can also act as metacommunicative procedures and as such
    serve to reinforce metalinguistic awareness in participants – a very useful
    function in ELF talk given the linguistic fragility of this genotypically
    multilingual discourse.

3. The third finding refers to the demonstration of solidarity and consensus,
    especially on the part of the Asian participants who, despite their topic
    recycling that led to monothematic monologues manage to cooperate, and
    co-construct utterances in a display of solidarity – the solidarity of non-
    native ELF speakers. In fact, collaborative, scaffolding discourse produc-
    tion is so frequent in this data that it may well be its most important feature.
    Interestingly, it is only the German speaker, who tried to pierce the bubble
    of apparent mutual intelligibility and overt collaboration. In her interview,
    the German speaker stated that she would prefer more argumentative talk,
    which can be interpreted as transfer of her German interactional preferences
    (House, 2003b).

The remarkable consensus orientation evident in this ELF data might be
interpreted with reference to Tajfel's (1981) assumption of a continuum of
interpersonal and group identity, such that one might posit a focus on group
identity. But the individual-group dichotomy may be too simplistic: Speakers
of L1s such as Korean, German, Indonesian and Chinese in my data are, when
using ELF, individuals who tend to transfer their L1 discourse conventions into
their ELF talk – while at the same time constructing something as fluid and

immaterial as the 'community of ELF speakers', a consortium that is always constituted anew in any ongoing talk.

In sum then, ELF users' native culture-conditioned ways of interacting are very much 'alive' in the medium of the English language; one might even speak of 'implicit translation' of L1 norms into ELF. Secondly, despite the resulting diversity of 'voices' in ELF – or maybe because using a common code for communication unites ELF speakers as non-native speakers ('We're all in the same boat') – ELF appears to be a useful egalitarian communicative tool that cannot be said to stunt speakers' interactional skills. While ELF users may need to improve their 'pragmatic fluency' (House, 2003c), their strategic competence is arguably intact, and it is this strategic competence which enables them to engage in meaningful, ordinary and robust ELF communication. In other words, ELF users cannot really be equated with 'reduced personalities': They are perfectly capable of holding their own in everyday talk.

The second major argument against using ELF in Europe relates to the claim that English 'contaminates' other European languages. I will try to relativise this claim by discussing the results of another project.

The Hamburg project 'covert translation'

Given the global use of ELF, one may wonder whether such spread may not lead to changes in the native local languages used alongside English. It is well-known that there has been a massive influx of English words, collocations, routines into many other languages. These lexical loans, which are most conspicuous in the media, advertising, life style or youth culture might well be brushed off as 'only' affecting the 'open system' of lexis leaving the 'heart of a language', its structure, intact. But what about the more hidden but much more serious influence of the English language on text and discourse norms in other languages? In a project funded by the German Science Foundation at its Center on Multilingualism (Baumgarten et al., 2004; House, 2004; House & Rehbein, 2004), we are currently investigating this very question, i.e. whether and how ELF influences textual norms in 'covert translation' and parallel text production. In a covert translation, the function of the original is maintained through the use of a 'cultural filter' with which culture-specific textual norms holding in the source language community are adapted to the norms in the receiving' community. Given ELF's impact on many domains of contemporary life in many countries, this adaptation process may now no longer take place. If this were the case, cross-cultural difference in text conventions would give way to anglophone ones, and a process would be initiated that might eventually result in cross-culturally similar processes of 'thinking for writing' (Slobin, 1996).

This hypothesis is tested using a diachronic translation and parallel text corpus of some 550 texts (800,000 words) from two genres: economics texts from globalised companies and popular science texts. The corpus is made up of three mutually contextualising parts: a primary corpus comprising original English texts and their translations into German, French and Spanish; a parallel corpus comprising authentic (i.e. non-translated) English and German texts; and a validation corpus holding translations from the same genres in the 'opposite direction', i.e. from German into English and translations from English into French and Spanish, as well as interviews with translators, editors, writers and other relevant persons. Initially we used a case study approach involving in-depth analysis and comparison of English originals and their translations as well as pairs of parallel texts on the basis of a translation model (House, 1997). Results of the analyses of some 80 translational pairs and parallel texts have at first disconfirmed our hypothesis, i.e. widespread borrowing of English lexical items and routines is not (yet) accompanied by changes in the make-up of texts in other languages. For instance, we found the same difference in the expression of 'interpersonal involvement' and in the degree of explicitness in describing events and states of affair between English and German texts which I had established earlier (cf. e.g. House, 1977). That this 'resistance' to English influence is a conscious one is evident from our interview data: the tendency towards humanising textual material in English popular science texts is deliberately shunned in favour of a more 'rational' or 'scientific' tenor in the German texts (which is deeply anchored in cultural tradition), i.e. a 'cultural filter' is applied as texts travel through time and space. Analyses of French and Spanish translations from English and corresponding parallel texts have yielded similar results. However, analyses of most recent textual specimens do now point to a change in the expression of 'subjectivity' or 'stance' and addressee orientation in German texts, and recent quantitative, diachronic research using two time frames (1978–1982 and 1999–2002) do indeed point to an incipient 'trend change' with respect to these domains, both of which belong to the interpersonal function of language, and are realised by phenomena such as speaker-hearer deixis and modality.

Given these new results, are we now in a position to claim that it is through language contact in translations from English and parallel text production that texts in other European languages become 'anglicised'? Our results cannot be described as confirming such a monocausal interpretation. Rather, they should be interpreted as leading to three possible explanations.

According to the first explanation, it is through translation that the dominance of the English language is promoted and spread. In the interaction between English textual norms and German textual norms in the process of translation, it is clearly English norms which overlay German ones, and this might eventually lead to language change. According to the second explanation, it is not the direct influence of the English language in the translational process, but rather its omnipresence in many domains of everyday life, and its global impact on the ways text producers conceive of and realise linguistically texts in particular genres. According to the third explanation, it is definitely *not* translations from English which propel anglophone influence on German textual norms, rather translators deliberately or unwittingly resist such influence and help retain language and culture specificity. In all three explanations – which can be seen as alternative explanatory hypotheses – developments over time are also indicated. It is likely, for instance, that special translated norms will develop in the translational process over time. Such considerations reflect the diachronic perspective pursued in the covert translation project described above.

In sum then, on the basis of the results of this project we cannot at the present time conclude that it is through the direct influence of the English language that text conventions in other languages change.

Whorfian perspectives

Proponents of Whorfian arguments claim that the massive import of English lexical items and routines inhibit and hijack entire domains of language use. This, they claim, will eventually lead to changes in speakers' formation of concepts in their L1 and, in an act of 'organised violence', force an anglophone Weltanschauung on speakers of other L1s, particularly in situations where content traditionally taught in learners' L1 is now taught in another language (mostly English) – a procedure currently promoted by EU institutions as CLIL (Content and Language Integrated Learning). Whorfians hold that (English language) CLIL scenarios are lethal to cognitive and conceptual development because they supplant the indigenous language. In the absence of controlled longitudinal studies it is difficult to support or reject such a claim. However, there is no need to believe in a wholesale mental and cognitive takeover by ELF as instructional language. Such a takeover would imply a strong Whorfian hypothesis, which we can reject without hesitation, firstly through pointing to the existence of translation, secondly using Ortega y Gasset's (1960) argument that our languages are but anachronisms and as such normally do not enter into our consciousness – if we are ordinary people that is, not poets, linguists, or language teachers given to non-ordinary linguistic sensitivities.

But what about the influence of large-scale instruction in ELF in tertiary education? Would not the fact that foreign students are taught not in the language of the land but in ELF do great damage to the international reputation of the local language and culture? This problem was tackled in a project recently completed at Hamburg University.

The project 'English as medium of instruction in German universities'

Motz (2005) has looked at how ELF as a medium of instruction in German universities interacts with the local German language and how international students interact in, and perceive this 'diglossic situation'. Using English in tertiary education is recognised as one dimension of 'anglification'. While such use of ELF was in the past most common in former British and American colonies, there are now attempts to use ELF in a European context, often in an attempt to 'internationalise' university curricula and attract more foreign students to Germany. Motz investigated how the fact that English is used in university and German in everyday life affects students' attitudes towards study, their domain-specific use of either language, and their assessment of this situation. Using a variety of qualitative research instruments, Motz found that students prefer a situation where the initial instruction in 'English only' is followed by a progression to German as the medium of instruction. This assessment of the needs and perceptions of those affected by the new 'two language situation' is in line with the official policy followed by the German Academic Exchange Service, where such a progression from ELF to German as the academic language is now favoured: Such a progression is thought to help increase the attractiveness of German as a language of science and as a useful tool for surviving in everyday life in the country chosen for study. English is seen as both a useful means of easing communication in initial stages and a useful stand-by for later situations involving, for instance, misunderstanding. There is then no real competition between German and English, the latter being in 'a class of its own', i.e. a supra-national means of communication.

Pedagogic perspectives

Europe's citizens, we are told, should be 'plurilingual', they should be taught their L1 plus two other European languages and, on top of this, I want to suggest, ELF. In EU documents such as the Council of Europe's 'Common European Framework of Reference for Languages', however, ELF's role in Europe is all but taboo. But the teaching of ELF need not take up much curricular time. Whereas other European languages might be taught as 'in depth languages', languages to be taught with their full cultural and historical background, ELF might be taught in much less time than 'in depth languages' that lend themselves for full philological teaching. If English is 'dealt with' early and efficiently as a *lingua franca* (cf. Jenkins, 2000; Seidlhofer, 2004), space and time is freed for other languages. Support for this idea comes e.g. from the Polish linguist Pfeiffer (1992), who demands a realistic assessment of the language situation in Europe and proposes a compromise solution: recognise explicitly the *de facto* function of English as an international communication medium and as a working language of the first choice, but also take all possible institutionalised steps to preserve, support and indeed extend Europe's traditional multilingualism and diversity. Instead of an unproductive and polemical 'either-or' situation we have a constructive 'both-and' one. The *de facto* special status of English in Europe needs to be officially recognised, and all other languages, especially indigenous and migrant minority languages, must be given special attention regionally and locally. If ELF is accepted as *sui generis*, other languages must then be vigorously supported (Nelde, 2003), i.e. positively discriminated by strong regional promotion, teaching and learning them as second, third etc. languages. If English were openly accepted as Europe's *lingua franca*, it would need to be taught intensively and early on as 'special case', and more time could then be allotted for other European languages in a flexible, differentiated, modularised fashion, tailor-made to regionally and locally differing needs.

A recent small-scale survey with East German language teachers, in which I elicited attitudes about the role of English in the schools and in Europe, revealed overwhelming support for using ELF in Europe. Most teachers thought accepting ELF for the EU facilitated communication and understanding and helped decrease costly competition among other European languages.

In another project, we are conducting narrative interviews with members of Germany's largest group of minority speakers: Turkish parents and their school age children. We are here eliciting attitudes towards, and experiences with, their multilingual life and school experiences; in particular with respect to learning English alongside German as L2 (or co-L1) and the Turkish L1, and attitudes towards the English language and its perceived communicative value. Preliminary results suggest that learning and using English is seen positively by most participants. Starting English 'after the German L2' gave Turkish children a feeling of being equal with the German children, who were also beginners in this case, and learning English meant becoming competent in a language with a high symbolic value.

In clear opposition to using ELF in Europe is the suggestion of preparing Europeans for a 'polyglot dialogue' put forward by the EuroCom project (Meissner, 2004), or the recommendation of 'semicommunication' e.g. between Scandinavian languages (Braunmüller, 2002). Both proposals imply that Europeans speak their mother tongues as often as possible and acquire 'passive competence' in as many European languages as possible. These suggestions are laudable, idealistic and probably well-meant. However, firstly they are unrealistic, as they demand in all of Europe mastery of a daunting array of languages, and secondly they ignore the world beyond Europe. Take the example of bicycle riding as opposed to driving a car: cycling is unquestionably better and healthier than sitting in a car. But despite this it is only feasible and indeed advisable in certain contexts. If you plan to go from Hamburg to say, Marbella, a car might be the better solution, but if you want to go to the local shops, take your bike! Again, an either-or solution to the question of ELF or diversity of languages in Europe is totally wrong: what we should be aiming for is a diversity and flexibility of foreign language learning and teaching goals depending on different individual goals, circumstances, constraints, and motivations.

Applied linguistics and English as a European lingua franca

I want to make three points about conceptualising and describing ELF for Europe which I see as a critically important task for the discipline of applied linguistics.

1. For ELF, the reductionist interlanguage framework, should be substituted by a social orientation towards language use. ELF's primary input does not come from native speakers but from a group of speakers who share a 'multilingual habitus'. Socially based models of language acquisition and use are in line with Russian theories of language learning, e.g. Galperin's (1980). In his cultural-historical 'interiorisation theory', psycholinguistic processes develop from and in interactions of the individual with other speakers in a variety of different contexts, such that events and states of affairs in the external world are 'taken inside' to build up schemata and construct mental realities.

2. The rejection of the psycholinguistic concept of an 'interlanguage' for ELF can find its parallel in the abandonment of the sociolinguistic concept of the 'speech community'. Since ELF speakers stem from heterogeneous backgrounds, come together with divergent social and linguistic expectations, and construct event-specific interactional styles and frameworks, a concept such as the 'community of practice' (Wenger, 1998) characterised by mutual engagement, joint negotiated enterprise, and shared repertoires of negotiable resources, is more adequate for descriptive and explanatory purposes.

3. Essential for conceptualising ELF communication is a radical rethinking of the linguistic norm against which speakers' competence is to be measured. Since ELF users are multilingual, this norm cannot be the monolingual native speaker, but rather an 'ELF expert'. While the conventional perspective on L2 speakers ignores their possession of other languages, the perspective on ELF speakers as a multilingual speakers

recognises the presence of other languages in ELF. For teaching and learning ELF, this means a revival of such undeservedly unfashionable activities as contrastive analyses on various levels of language as well as such classic language contact tasks as translation and interpreting.

Conclusion

The spread of English has invoked fears of linguistic uniformity and inequality, and has provoked strong resistance coupled with an emergent pride in national, regional and local languages. In becoming more and more pluralised, English has accommodated ELF speakers' diverse needs and values. For the description of this situation, 'a third way' is necessary in between the two extremes of fighting the spread of ELF for its linguistic imperialism and uncritically accepting ELF for its cultural and linguistic neutrality. Such a third way would emphasise ELF's inherent hybridity and its function as a 'co-language' alongside local languages to serve speakers' own communicative needs.

What makes many of us so angry about global English has probably not much to do with language at all. It has to do with the fact that global English is often associated with global American business power. Language is but an instrument with which this power is used, and the result is often an exasperating sameness, which, as Cameron (2000) points out, has come to be Europe's language of service via such global players as McDonalds. To counteract such sameness, we must re-instate the particular, the local, the special, the individual and re-contextualise global linguistic behaviour to prevent further inroads of an anonymous *passe partout* style. For this we need less lofty academic theorising of the 'ecology of language' type, but more modest localised research. This is what Edward Said might have meant in the afterword to the 1995 edition of his *Orientalism*, where he points to the importance of the disposition of power and powerlessness in society, which is more than academic wool-gathering. Sadly, the growing interest of academics in multiculturalism and post-colonialism can in fact be interpreted as an intellectual retreat from the new realities of massive global power. Rather than academic gesture, talk and writing only, we do however need rigorous analysis of the problems on hand, as well as firm stance-taking followed by action to combat the type of self-deception and scientific distraction in which academics all too often engage to soothe their conscience. What applied linguists, who are more closely bound to what happens in 'the real world' than many other professionals, should be doing is revealing injustice and oppression. This is where the real challenge lies.

References

Baumgarten, N. J., House, J. and Probst, J. (2004) English as lingua franca in covert translation processes. *The Translator* 10: 183–08.

Bisong, J. (1995) Language choice and cultural imperialism: a Nigerian perspective. *ELT Journal* 49: 122–67.

Bloch, J. (2004) Second language cyber rhetoric: a study of Chinese L2 writers in an online usenet group. *Language Learning & Technology* 8(3): 66–82.

Braunmüller, K. (2002) Semicommunication and accommodation: observations from the linguistic situation in Scandinavia. *International Journal of Applied Linguistics* 12: 1–23.

Cameron, D. (2000) *Good to Talk?* London: Sage.

Cook, V. (1993) *Linguistics and Second Language Acquisition*. New York: St. Martin's Press.

Edmondson, W. J. (1981) *Spoken Discourse. A Model for Analysis*. London: Longman.

Firth, A. (1996) The discursive accomplishment of normality. On 'lingua franca' English and conversation analysis. *Journal of Pragmatics* 26: 237–60.

Galperin, P. (1980) *Zu Grundfragen der Psychologie*. Berlin: Verlag Volk und Wissen.

Gramkow Andersen, K. (1993) *Lingua Franca Discourse: an investigation of the use of English in an international business context*. MA Thesis, Aalborg.

Grosjean, F. (2001) The bilingual's language mode. In J. L.Nicol (ed.) *Language Processing in the Bilingual*. Oxford: Blackwell.

House, J. (1977) *A Model for Translation Quality Assessment*. Tübingen: Narr.

House, J. (1997) *Translation Quality Assessment: a model revisited*. Tübingen: Narr.

House, J. (2002) Communicating in English as a lingua franca. In S. Foster-Cohen (ed.) *EUROSLA Yearbook 2* 243–61. Amsterdam: Benjamins.

House, J. (2003a) English as a lingua franca: a threat to multilingualism? *Journal of Sociolinguistics* 7(4): 556–78.

House, J. (2003b) Misunderstanding in intercultural university encounters. In J. House et al. (eds) 22–56.

House, J. (2003c) Teaching and learning pragmatic fluency in a foreign language: the case of English as a lingua franca. In A. Martinez-Flor, E. Usó Juan, A. Fernandez Guerra (eds) *Pragmatic Competence and Foreign Language Teaching* 133–160. Castellon: U. Jaume I.

House, J. (2004) English as a lingua franca and its influence on texts in other European languages. In G. Garzone and A. Cardinaletti (eds) *Lingua, Mediazione e Interferenza* 21–48. Milano: Franco Angeli.

House, J., Kasper, G. and Ross, S. (eds) (2003) *Misunderstanding in Social Life*. London: Longman.

House, J. and Rehbein, J. (eds) (2004) *Multilingual Communication*. Amsterdam: Benjamins.

Hüllen, W. (1992) Identifikationssprachen und Kommunikationssprachen. *Zeitschrift für Germanistische Linguistik* 20: 298–317.

Jenkins, J. (2000) *The Phonology of English as an International Language.* Oxford: Oxford University Press.

Koskinen, K. (2000) Translating in the EU Commission. *The Translator* 6: 49–66.

Lam, W. S. E. (2004) Second language socialization in a bilingual chatroom: global and local considerations. *Language Learning & Technology* 8(3): 44–65.

Lesznyák, Á. (2004) *Communication in English as an International Lingua Franca.* Norderstedt: Books on Demand.

Meissner, F.-J. (2004) Modelling plurilingual processing and language growth between intercomprehensive languages In L. Zybatow (ed.) *Translation in der globalen Welt und neue Wege der Sprach- und Übersetzer Ausbildung* 225–42. Frankfurt/Main: Lang

Motz, M. (2005) *Ausländische Studierende in Internationalen Studiengängen: Motivation, Sprachverwendung und sprachliche Bedürfnisse.* Bochum: AKS Verlag.

Nelde, H. P. (2003) Die Zukunft hat schon begonnen – Minderheiten im werdenden Europa. In J. Besters-Dilger et al. (eds) *Mehrsprachigkeit in der erweiterten Europäischen Union* 28–43. Klagenfurt: Drava.

Ortega y Gasset, J. (1960) *Miseria y Esplendor de la Traduccion.* (Third edition) Ebenhausen: Langewiessche-Brandt.

Pfeiffer, W. (1992) Eine Sprache für alle oder für jeden eine? Ein Essay aus der Sicht eines Polen. *Die Neueren Sprachen* 30: 429–52.

Seidlhofer, B. (2004) Research perspectives on teaching English as a lingua franca. *Annual Review of Applied Linguistics* 24: 209–42.

Selinker, L. (1972) Interlanguage. *IRAL* 10: 209–30.

Slobin, D. (1996) From 'thought and language' to 'thinking for speaking'.' In J. Gumperz and S. Levinson (eds) *Rethinking Linguistic Relativity* 70–96. Cambridge: Cambridge University Press.

De Swaan, A. (2001) *Words of the World.* Oxford: Polity.

Tajfel, H. (1981) *Human Groups and Social Categories.* Cambridge: Cambridge University Press.

Watts, R. (2001) Discourse theory and language planning: a critical reading of language planning reports in Switzerland. In N. Coupland et al. (eds) *Sociolinguistics and Social Theory* 297–320. London: Longman.

Wenger, E. (1998) *Communities of Practice.* Cambridge: Cambridge University Press.

Widdowson, H. (2003) *Defining Issues in English Language Teaching.* Oxford: Oxford University Press.

7 Data-driven learning in German for academic purposes: a corpus-based approach for specialist learners

Dr Martina Möllering

Abstract

Following the rationale that corpora have an important part to play in fostering language awareness, this paper investigates the use of corpora in the teaching of German as a foreign language. Over the past decade, corpus-based research has had an increasing influence on language teaching pedagogy (cf. Tribble & Jones, 1989; Johns & King, 1991; Wichmann et al., 1997; Kennedy, 1998; McEnery & Wilson, 2001). While the majority of studies reporting on corpus-based teaching approaches refer to English, only a small number of studies have discussed such an approach for German (e.g. Dodd, 1997; Jones, 1997; Möllering, 2001). This paper describes an approach to teaching German designed for students who wish to acquire a reading knowledge of the German language, specifically for research purposes in the field of Ancient History where a large number of standard texts are published in German. The paper discusses the design and compilation of a corpus of German academic texts, which serves as a basis for linguistic analysis of semantic, morphological and syntactic patterns through procedures commonly employed in corpus analysis, such as compilation of word lists, frequency counts and concordances. While existing corpora of written German focus mainly on press and literary texts, a specialised corpus as examined here can serve as a database for research into the linguistic structures particular to academic texts in German, notably in the domain of Ancient History. In this contribution, the exploitation of language corpora is proposed in order to arrive at authentic teaching materials in the field of German for Academic Purposes.

Introduction: principles and methodologies of corpus-based research

Corpus-based research has had an increasing influence on language teaching pedagogy, with regard to linguistic content as well as to teaching methodology. Kennedy (1998: 281/2) outlines the potential influence of a corpus-based approach on language teaching as follows:

> For those concerned with the teaching and learning of second or foreign languages in particular, information on the distribution of the elements and processes of a language can influence pedagogy in a number of ways. First it can influence the content of language teaching by affecting selection of what to teach, the sequencing of pedagogy, and the weight given to items or parts of the language being taught, thus contributing directly to the content of instruction. Secondly, through the consciousness raising of teachers about language and language use, it can show that likelihood of occurrence, or frequency of use, is an important measure of usefulness. Corpus studies can also contribute to language teaching methodology by influencing the approach to instruction and making available techniques and procedures which encourage self-access and individualized instruction through interaction with authentic, analyzed text from a corpus database.

In this study, a corpus-based approach is proposed with regard to the content as well as with regard to the methodology aspect of language teaching as described by Kennedy above. Before referring in detail to the present study, the principles and methodologies of a corpus-based approach are briefly discussed.

Corpus linguistics (e.g. Aarts & Meijs 1984; Aijmer & Altenberg, 1991; Biber, Conrad & Reppen, 1998; Kennedy, 1998; McEnery & Wilson, 2001; Sinclair, 1991; Svartvik, 1992; Thomas & Short, 1996) as a method of enquiry in linguistics is of an empirical nature. In very simple terms, it can be described as the study of language based on examples of language use in real life. Advances in computing technology have made it possible to store large amounts of language data referred to as corpora.

A corpus is a principled collection of texts, i.e. when compiling a corpus a number of considerations are taken into account. A distinction is made, for instance, between general corpora and specialised corpora (e.g. dialect corpora, non-standard corpora, learners' corpora). A general corpus is usually assembled to form a base for unspecified linguistic research. To be considered representative of the language it exemplifies, such a corpus is typically balanced, i.e. it contains texts from different domains and genres, including spoken and written, private and public language, etc. Balanced or general corpora are also named core corpora (cf. Kennedy, 1998: 20) and can be used as a basis for comparative study in contrast with specialised corpora. How representative a corpus is depends in part on the way it has been sampled and in part on its size. A general corpus attempts to capture the scope of linguistic variation which is present in a language. This requires a stratified approach (Biber et al., 1998), which catalogues the different categories of texts in a language and samples each of them. An important question is how the categorisation criteria have been arrived at, i.e. which situational characteristics were used to define registers (for a more detailed discussion of sampling see McEnery & Wilson, 2001: 77ff).

As there are important differences in the use of grammatical, lexical and discourse features across different varieties of language, a general corpus needs to represent this diversity (Biber et al., 1998: 248):

> Several areas are important to consider for diversity. Prime among them is register variation. Register variation is central to language: all speakers of a language control many registers, and every time people speak or write, they must choose a register to use ... A well-designed corpus must therefore represent the different registers of the language.

The size of a corpus is often ascribed in terms of finite size as represented by a total number of words (e.g. 100,000,000 words for the British National Corpus). Such a corpus may be referred to as a static corpus (cf. Kennedy, 1998), which is compiled up to a certain size or date and then not amended any further. In contrast to static corpora, dynamic (Kennedy, 1998) or monitor corpora (Sinclair, 1991) are constantly added to, not necessarily in the balanced way described above. An unofficial standard for electronic corpora (of the general kind as described above) used to be around the one million word mark until the early 1990s. Nowadays, much larger corpora, like the Bank of English with 400,000,000 words (McEnery & Wilson, 2001) are becoming available. Although the spoken language is the more common mode of use, most corpus-based studies of language so far have been carried out on written language, as the amount of time and effort necessary to create a sizeable corpus of spoken language is far greater than for the written language. Transcriptions of spoken language data are time-consuming, especially when phonetic and prosodic features are included.

The majority of corpus-based studies have so far been carried out on the English language, as a large body of sizeable corpora is available for different varieties of English, but more and more languages are being researched with the help of corpora (McEnery & Wilson, 2001: 188):

> [In 1996], work had begun on corpora of western and eastern European languages. It seemed that corpus linguistics was expanding to cover Europe (on projects such as BABEL, CRATER and MULTEXT) and English

speaking countries (ICE)... In an amazingly short period of time – in essence the 1990s – corpus linguistics has spread to cover a large number of world languages.

Corpus-based research has investigated the use of language features in areas such as lexicography, grammar, lexico-grammar and discourse characteristics as well as characteristics of language varieties. Thus, the focus is either on the use of a linguistic feature, lexical and/or grammatical, or on the characteristics of texts or varieties. Corpus-based analyses explore associations of the feature under investigation as summarised by Biber et al. (1998: 6) in the following overview:

Association Patterns in Language Use

A. Investigating the use of a linguistic feature (lexical or grammatical)

    (i)   Linguistic associations of the feature

                - lexical associations (associations with particular words)

                - grammatical associations (associations with particular grammatical constructions)

    (ii)   Non-linguistic associations of the feature

                - distribution across registers

                - distributions across dialects

                - distribution across time periods

B. Investigating varieties or texts (e.g. registers, dialects, historical periods)

    (i)   Linguistic association patterns

                - individual linguistic features or classes of features

                - co-occurrence patterns of linguistic features

The analysis of corpora is usually carried out as an interaction between human processing, computer processing and corpus data. Leech (1991: 14) describes this interaction in the following way:

> There are a number of ways in which human, software and corpus resources can interact, according to how far the human analyst delegates to the computer the responsibility for analysis. At one end of the scale, the computer program (e.g. concordance program) is used simply as a tool for sorting and counting data, while all the serious analysis is performed by the human investigator. ... At the other extreme, the human analyst provides no

linguistic insight, just programming ability; the machine discovers its own categories of analysis, in effect implementing a 'discovery procedure'.

Between these two ends of the scale lie a number of procedures which result from the interaction between human analysis and computer analysis. In order to facilitate the analysis of large machine-readable corpora, these are commonly annotated. Annotation criteria are in a first step developed on the basis of human analysis, then fed back into computer programmes, so that the annotation can be carried out automatically by the machine. Annotation, the enhancement of a corpus with various types of linguistic information, makes explicit what is implicit information in the language forms represented in the corpus. Typical forms of annotation include lemmatisation, tagging and parsing (for a detailed description of annotation procedures see McEnery & Wilson, 2001: 32ff). The corpus described in the present study was not annotated.

Common procedures used in corpus analysis include the compilation of word lists, frequency counts and concordances. Concordancing software typically produces KWIC (Key Word In Context) files or concordances, in which the key word appears in the centre of the line, with its co-text to the left and right. The co-text contains immediate and less immediate col-locates so that collocation can be studied with the help of the concordancing software. The file can be sorted in various ways, e.g. alphabetically by the first or second word to the right or left, so that recurring patterns can be illuminated. The frequency of a key word or collocate can be established and, for instance, be used for comparisons between text types or – as e.g. Kennedy (1998) proposed – to establish how salient a linguistic feature is for the language learner.

Corpora of German and corpus-based teaching of German

The aim of this project was to create a specialised corpus of academic German in the field of Ancient History. Although there are numerous corpora of written German – in particular those held by the 'Institute for the German Language' (IDS) in Mannheim, Germany, with about 1080 million words of which 653 million words are publicly accessible via the data retrieval system COSMAS (IDS, 2004) – as yet there exists no such specialised corpus as proposed here. The existing corpora of written German focus mainly on press and literary texts and contain only a small proportion of academic texts from the Sciences as well as the Humanities.

While the majority of studies reporting on corpus-based teaching approaches refer to English (e.g. Fligelstone, 1993; Biber et al., 1994; Wichmann et al., 1997; Conrad, 2000) a number of studies have discussed

German. Dodd (1997) reports on exploiting a corpus of written German for advanced language learning, using the 'Bonner Zeitungskorpus' (Bonn Newspaper Corpus), which is held by the 'Institut für Deutsche Sprache' (IDS) in Mannheim and has just over three million words of running text. Students access the corpus using MicroConcord (Scott & Johns, 1993) through the university's computer network. Dodd (ibid.) discusses three ways of exploiting unedited data: as an informal resource for students to browse through, as a resource for formulating explicit grammatical knowledge and as a resource for student-led projects on grammatical or sociolinguistic topics. Jones (1997) compiled a corpus of spoken German of about 600,000 words, which he uses with students of German at Brigham Young University. Students can access the corpus through the college network and work on a given assignment, which, in a first step, is usually a single word. They analyse the word, as it occurs in the corpus, then compare the analysis with a German-English dictionary, a standard German reference grammar and with a beginning and intermediate textbook for learning German. Jones (1997: 154) reports that students have found grammatical functions of words which are sometimes not explained in reference grammars. Jones (ibid.) points out that it is useful for students to learn the relative frequency of various functions of a word. Möllering (2001) proposes the use of corpus-based materials for the teaching of German modal particles, drawing on the quantitative analysis of a collection of corpora of spoken German held at the *Institut für Deutsche Sprache* (*Freiburger Korpus*, *Dialogstrukturenkorpus*, and *Pfeffer-Korpus*) and the qualitative analysis of a corpus of telephone conversations using MicroConcord (Scott & Johns, 1993). Following a detailed corpus-based linguistic analysis of the particle *eben* she provides a sample worksheet to demonstrate how such an analysis can be incorporated into language teaching.

In the context of the present study, the exploitation of a language corpus is proposed in order to arrive at authentic teaching materials which facilitate the comprehension of German academic writing in the field of Ancient History. Leech (1997) distinguishes between the direct use of corpora in teaching and the use of corpora indirectly applied to teaching. Teaching about corpora, teaching the exploitation of corpora and exploiting corpora to teach are said to represent a direct use of corpora, whereas reference publishing, materials development and language testing are indirect applications (Leech, 1997: 6-7). Following Leech's distinction, the approach proposed here is direct in that it exploits a specialist corpus of German described below to arrive at relevant data.

Creation of a specialist learners' corpus

In the Australian context, the past decade has seen a shift from students entering tertiary German courses with Higher School Certificate qualifications to students with no or a very limited knowledge of the language, so that introductory German courses have become those with the strongest enrolment figures (cf. Lutzeier, 1998, for developments in other English speaking countries). While the majority of these language units are directed at teaching communicative competence incorporating the four skills of reading and writing, speaking and listening, there is a need for more specifically oriented courses, particularly in German, in the area of reading for academic purposes. At the university, where the project described here is based, this perceived need for reading units in German lies particularly in the field of Ancient History, where such units have attracted stable and relatively strong enrolments in the past, mainly by postgraduate students. The teaching materials for German reading units that are available commercially (e.g. Roche, 2000; Jannach & Korb, 1998; Coles & Dodd, 1997; Wilson, 1996; Rogalla & Rogalla, 1985) are not specific to this subject area and the development of an area-specific teaching approach has been the starting point for the current project.

The aim was to create a course that would take a more learner-centred approach to reading knowledge based on authentic texts from the subject area and supported by an online component. Part of the course was to be a corpus of German academic texts, which could serve as the basis for the linguistic analysis of semantic, as well as morphological and syntactic patterns. This paper focuses on the compilation of such a specialist corpus and its possible applications.

A specialised corpus of the kind discussed here may serve as a database for research into and teaching of the linguistic structures particular to academic texts in German. The domain under discussion in this contribution is ancient history, a field in which a large number of standard texts are written in German, making it necessary for ancient history scholars to gain a reading knowledge of the German language. Such a corpus will provide a database for researching properties of academic German in this domain under semantic aspects (e.g. Frequency of particular lexical items), morphological aspects (e.g. Morphological patterns of noun composition) and syntactic aspects (e.g. Nominal versus verbal structures).

In a first step, a body of texts to be compiled for the database had to be identified. To this end, questionnaires were devised and sent to the following groups of specialists in the field:

- Students in the German reading units
- Postgraduate students in Ancient History
- Academic staff in Ancient History (at Macquarie University and affiliated staff at US and British universities)

In the questionnaire, staff and students in Ancient History were asked to identify texts that they used in their teaching and research under the following categories:

- Specialist journals
- Standard reference books
- Introductions
- Monographs
- Site reports
- Catalogues
- Edited works/collection of articles
- Dictionaries (ancient language into German)
- Grammar books
- Translations and commentaries of ancient text
- Travel guides

The questionnaires were then evaluated according to text type and content categories and an assessment of the online availability of texts was carried out.

To date, only texts available online in a downloadable format have been used with a proportion of not more than one article per online journal and one chapter per online book to achieve a balance in the composition of the corpus, but also to conform with the university's copyright guidelines. The current size of the corpus is approximately 300,000 words.

Corpus-based teaching in German for special purposes

Procedures used in corpus analysis include the compilation of word lists, frequency counts and concordances. Word lists compiled on the basis of the corpus discussed here will be used as the starting point for a glossary that is to be part of the online unit and will be accessible to students enrolled in the course. Concordances based on the selection of texts in the corpus will feed into the teaching materials as a source for paradigms of lexical and grammatical collocations and as the base for explorative tasks to be solved by the learners. In the following paragraphs, a number of examples of such concordances will illustrate their possible applications for teaching.

Concordancing software is used to produce KWIC files or concordances, in which the key word appears in the centre of the line, with its co-text to the left and right. The co-text contains immediate and less immediate collocates so that collocation can be analysed with the help of the concordancing software. The file can be sorted in various ways, e.g. alphabetically by the first or second word to the right or left, so that recurring patterns can be illuminated. The association patterns which are of particular interest in the context of teaching German reading skills are linguistic associations of a particular linguistic feature, where we can further distinguish between lexical associations, i.e. associations with particular words, and grammatical associations, i.e. association with particular grammatical constructions (cf. Biber et al., 1998). The following examples of concordances are drawn from 30,000 word samples of the corpus compiled in this project. They provide an illustration of the different kinds of association patterns that can be elucidated by a corpus-based linguistic analysis.

Lexical association

The first example is a concordance that investigates the use of a certain lexical feature, namely the verb *handeln*, which is commonly translated as:

(a) to trade
(b) to bargain, to haggle
(c) to act
(d) to behave
(e) to deal with something (with preposition *von* or *über*)

A search for *handel** – with * indicating that all forms of the verb (present and past, singular and plural forms) were to be included – yielded the following concordance:

Concordance for *handel** (15 lines)

```
 1 m es zu einem schwungvollen Handel mit Mumien, die in großer
 2 iches methodisches Postulat handeln mag, so scheint seine Umse
 3  tpaulinischen Denkens und Handelns vor dem Hintergrund antik
 4 e Einstellung des sozialen Handelns [a] auf subjektiv gef hlt
 5 e Vernunft.Zur Theorie des Handelns, Frankfurt/M. 1998, 163-1
 6 Korinth nachweisen, jedoch handelt es sich hierbei nur um ein
 7 eziehungen dienen. Demnach handelt es sich bei Patron-Klient-
 8 ch um Güter und Leistungen handelt, dieso unterschiedlicher N
 9  mit welchem Status es sich handelt, da wir über ihre Rolle, F
10 rbindung bringen 54 .Dabei handelt es sich um ein aus der Kul
11 riert werden. Auch hierbei handelt es sich um Zusatzannahmen
12 n durchaus verdienen.Dabei handelt es sich um zwei Gruppen vo
13 diesem Balsamierungsritual handelt es sich gleichsam um ein r
```

```
14 re abgeleitet werden, noch handelte es sich um eine daranorie
15 rn allt gliche Beziehungen handelte, die besonders dort eine
```

Amongst the different forms of the verb *handeln*, we also find four occurrences of the word as noun (lines 1, 3, 4, 5) evidenced by the capital spelling of the word within a clause. The verb appears once in its infinitival form (line 2), but mainly occurs as a third-person singular form, either in present tense (lines 6–13) or in past tense (lines 14 and 15). So much for a grammatical analysis of the occurrences – what is potentially of more interest to beginning readers of German, however, is an analysis of lexical collocation in those few lines. In the following concordance, the occurrences have been right-sorted, and we can see a pattern emerging, in the newly numbered lines 5–11:

Concordance for *handel** – right-sorted

```
1    e Einstellung des sozialen Handelns [a] auf subjektiv gefühlt
2     mit welchemStatus es sich handelt, da wir über ihre Rolle, F
3    rn alltägliche Beziehungen handelte, die besondersdort eine b
4    ch um Güter und Leistungen handelt, die so unterschiedlicher N
5    eziehungen dienen. Demnach handelt es sich bei Patron-Klient-
6    diesem Balsamierungsritual handelt es sich gleichsam um ein r
7    Korinth nachweisen, jedoch handelt es sich hierbei nur um eine
8    re abgeleitet werden, noch handelte es sich um eine daran orie
9    riert werden. Auch hierbei handelt es sich um Zusatzannahmen
10   n durchaus verdienen.Dabei handelt es sich um zwei Gruppen vo
11   rbindung bringen 54 .Dabei handelt es sich um ein aus der Kul
12   e Vernunft.Zur Theorie des Handelns, Frankfurt/M. 1998, 163-1
13   ches methodisches Postulat handeln mag, so scheint seine Umse
14    es zu einem schwungvollen Handel mit Mumien, die in großer Z
15   ätpaulinischen Denkens und Handelns vor dem Hintergrund antik
```

Here, the task for a reader of German is to identify the collocation of the verb *handeln* with the pronoun *es*, the reflexive pronoun *sich* and the preposition *um*, where the verb takes on a very different meaning from the ones given above, namely:

'To be about sth', 'to concern sth'

```
5    eziehungen dienen. Demnach handelt es sich bei Patron-Klient-
6    diesem Balsamierungsritual handelt es sich gleichsam um ein r
7    Korinth nachweisen, jedoch handelt es sich hierbei nur um eine
8    re abgeleitet werden, noch handelte es sich um eine daran orie
9    riert werden. Auch hierbei handelt es sich um Zusatzannahmen
```

```
10   n durchaus verdienen.Dabei handelt es sich um zwei Gruppen vo
11   rbindung bringen 54 .Dabei handelt es sich um ein aus der Kul
```

Another example for lexical association can be seen in the following concordance for the word *Frage*, meaning 'question':

Concordance for *Frage* (33 lines)

```
1    iffen werden:Zum einen die Frage nach dem Verhältnis zwischen
2    Gemeinde, zum anderen die Frage, nach welchen Kriterien die
3    flikte, besonders aber die Frage nach der Stellung der Aposte
4    Marshall 10 nimmt bei der Frage nach den Gründen für die Pau
5    fen. Damit stellt sich die Frage, inwieweit die Erkenntnisse
6    dargestellt werden, um der Frage nachgehen zu können, ob die
7    einem nächsten Schritt der Frage nachgegangen, ob und wie sic
8    h einmal grundsätzlich die Frage aufzuwerfen, welchen heurist
9    nage erklären lassen.Diese Frage kann hier zun chst nur in se
10   haben. Schlagend ist Holls Frage (61) hinsichtlich der prophe
11   ist. Dann stellt sich die Frage, ob man sich einen Amtsträge
12   c) Es stellt sich noch die Frage nach dem Institutionalisieru
13   t sich das Problem auf die Frage, ob Paulus das römische Bürg
14   ZNW 78, 1987, 200-229. Die Frage des Bürgerrechts desPaulus k
15   gl. A.J.M. Wedderburn, Zur Frage der Gattung der Apostelgesch
16   ging es um die allgemeine Frage des Verhältnisses zwischen d
17   ar, die für diese Rolle in Frage käme.Innerhalb der Ortsgemei
18   r zuerw hnen: Zunächst die Frage nach dem Ausschluß des Unzu
19   nders(1Kor 5), sodann die Frage der (rechtlichen) Streitbeil
20   n(1Kor 6,1-8), ferner die Frage nach der Gültigkeit von Spei
21   8-10) und schließlich die Frage nach der Praxis der christli
22   t hätte 75 . Auch wenn die Frage aus dem gegebenen Material l
23   ist.Auch in bezug auf die Frage des Rechtsstreits zwischen z
24   g zu wählen. Wirft man die Frage auf, wer auch wegen einerkle
25   -resignativ zu verstehende Frage des Paulus, ob denn agar kei
26   cherweise in bezug auf die Frage der Abhaltung christlicher T
27   . Diesbezüglich bleibt die Frage, ob die größere Anzahl klein
28   Zuvor stellt sich noch die Frage, wie man sich einen christli
29   me.Sodann stellt sich die Frage, welchen heuristischen Statu
30   gen haben kann. Gerade die Frage, wie und warum die apostolis
31   aus irgend einem Grund in Frage gestellt bzw. herausgeforder
32   en sollen, stellt sich die Frage, ob es ihn denn nun eigentli
33   ttelmeer beantwortet diese Frage. Aus der bei Assuan liegende
```

In 8 out of the 33 occurrences above, the word *Frage* collocates with the preposition *nach*, mostly in the construction:

article + *Frage* + *nach* + article 'the question about/of'

Proximity match for *nach* (8 lines)

```
1    c) Es stellt sich noch die Frage nach dem Institutionalisieru
2    iffen werden:Zum einen die Frage nach dem Verhältnis zwischen
3    r zuerwähnen: Zunächst die Frage nach dem Ausschluß des Unzuc
4    Marshall 10 nimmt bei der Frage nach den Gründen für die Pau
5    r Gemeinde,zum anderen die Frage,nach welchen Kriterien die
6    en(1Kor 6,1-8), ferner die Frage nach der Gültigkeit von Spei
7    flikte, besonders aber die Frage nach der Stellung der Aposte
8    8-10) und schließlich die Frage nach der Praxis der christli
```

The two brief examples above illustrate how a corpus-based approach using concordancing procedures can illuminate lexical association patterns which occur frequently in the specialist texts under discussion. Being able to identify those lexical chunks enables beginning readers of German to access meaning much more quickly and accurately than a word-for-word translation procedure would allow them to do.

Grammatical association

In the following concordance the keyword is the article *des*, which is the genitive form of the masculine definite article in German.

Concordance for *des*

```
1    kian abgeleiteter Idealtyp des aristokratischen Hauses find
2    en war und mit dem Zerfall des achäischen Bundes unter römisch
3    ericht. Oststadt: Bebauung des Alten Reiches, in:MDAIK 43, 19
4    s. (Hg.), Max Webers Sicht des antiken Christentums.Interpret
5    nschaften häufige Betonung des antilegalistischen Aspekts ein
6    sia)20 . Eine Besonderheit des christlichen Gemeindebegriffs
7    e Mitte derfünfziger Jahre des ersten Jahrhunderts nicht zule
8    che, da Paulus gegen Ende des ersten Korintherbriefes forder
9    die Form eines Skarabäus, des heiligen Mistkäfers der Ägypte
10   und Feuerböcke. Jahresber. des Historischen Museums in Bern 1
11   t. Studien zur Entwicklung des kollektiven Bewußtseins in der
```

The concordance presented here is a selection of those occurrences of *des* which are immediately followed by an adjective and a noun. Such a concordance would lend itself to help the beginning reader of German identify the grammatical collocation of the article form *des* with a particular ending to the following adjective and noun:

Des + ...en + ...(e)s

thus establishing the grammatical rule for identifying a noun phrase in the genitive case:

Concordance for *des*

```
1    kian abgeleiteter Idealtyp des aristokratischen Hauses find
2    en war und mit dem Zerfall des achäischen Bundes unter römisch
3    ericht. Oststadt: Bebauung des Alten Reiches, in:MDAIK 43, 19
4    s. (Hg.), Max Webers Sicht des antiken Christentums.Interpret
5     nschaften häufige Betonung des antilegalistischen Aspekts ein
6    sia)20 . Eine Besonderheit des christlichen Gemeindebegriffs
7    e Mitte derfünfziger Jahre des ersten Jahrhunderts nicht zule
8     che, da Paulus gegen Ende des ersten Korintherbriefes forder
9     die Form eines Skarabäus, des heiligen Mistkäfers der Ägypte
10   und Feuerböcke. Jahresber. des Historischen Museums in Bern 1
11   t. Studien zur Entwicklung des kollektiven Bewußtseins in der
```

The scope of this article does not allow for a detailed description of the development of teaching materials. Concordances such as the ones provided as examples above can be used either as explorative tasks where learners study the concordance to discover lexical and/or grammatical collocations and subsequently establish tenets about grammatical patterns and patterns of meaning. Alternatively, concordances might be turned into gap-exercises, where the task for the learner is to establish the key word that is missing (for an overview of teaching with concordances see e.g. Tribble & Jones, 1990; Johns & King, 1991; Thurstun & Candlin, 1997; for an example of a worksheet based on concordancing see e.g. Möllering, 2001). It should suffice here to provide an example of a worksheet, based on one of the analyses demonstrated above, to illustrate a concordance-based task.

Sample worksheet: des

The following examples show the word *des* in context. Please underline the noun phrases following *des* in those examples:

```
1    kian abgeleiteter Idealtyp des aristokratischen Hauses find
2    en war und mit dem Zerfall des achäischen Bundes unter römisch
```

```
 3    ericht. Oststadt: Bebauung des Alten Reiches, in:MDAIK 43, 19
 4    s. (Hg.), Max Webers Sicht des antiken Christentums.Interpret
 5     nschaften häufige Betonung des antilegalistischen Aspekts ein
 6    sia)20 . Eine Besonderheit des christlichen Gemeindebegriffs
 7    Mitte der fünfziger Jahre des ersten Jahrhunderts nicht zule
 8    che, da Paulus gegen Ende des ersten Korintherbriefes forder
 9    die Form eines Skarabäus, des heiligen Mistkäfers der Ägypte
10    und Feuerböcke. Jahresber. des Historischen Museums in Bern 1
11    t. Studien zur Entwicklung des kollektiven Bewußtseins in der
```

Now have a look at the endings of the adjectives and nouns in those phrases.
What is the pattern of endings following the article *des*?
Adjectives end in   _____
Nouns end in   _____

The following phrases are based on the sample line above. Please compare
them to the German book titles in your bibliographies. Can you find the same
kind of pattern there?

> *Der Idealtyp* des *aristokratischen Hauses*
> *Der Zerfall* des *achäischen Bundes*
> *Die Bebauung* des *Alten Reiches*
> *Die Betonung* des *antilegalistischen Aspekts*
> *Die Entwicklung* des *kollektiven Bewußtseins*

References

Aarts, J. and Meijs, W. (eds) (1984) *Corpus Linguistics*. Amsterdam: Rodopi.

Aijmer, K. and Altenberg, B. (eds) (1991) *English Corpus Linguistics*: *studies in honour of Jan Svartvik*. London/New York: Longman.

Biber, D., Conrad, S. and Reppen, R. (1994) Corpus-based approaches to issues in applied linguistics. *Applied Linguistics* 15(2): 169–89.

Biber, D., Conrad, S. and Reppen, R. (1998) *Corpus Linguistics. Investigating language structure and use*. Cambridge: Cambridge University Press.

British National Corpus. http://www.natcorp.ox.ac.uk/

Coles, W. and Dodd, B. (1997) *Reading German. A course book and reference grammar*. New York: Oxford University Press.

Conrad, S. (2000) Will corpus linguistics revolutionize grammar teaching in the 21st century? *TESOL Quarterly* 34(3): 548–60.

Dodd, B. (1997). Exploiting a corpus of written German for advanced language learning. In A. Wichmann, S. Fligelstone, T. McEnery and G. Knowles (eds) *Teaching and Language Corpora* 131–45. London/New York: Longman.

Dodd, B. (ed.) (2000) *Working with German Corpora*. Birmingham: Birmingham University Press.

Fligelstone, S. (1993) Some reflections on the question of teaching, from a corpus linguistics perspective. *ICAME Journal* 17: 97–109.

Institut für deutsche Sprache. (2004) *COSMAS*. http://www.ids-mannheim. de/cosmas2/

Jannach, H. and Korb, R. (1998) *German for Reading Knowledge*. Boston: Heinle & Heinle.

Johns, T. and King, P. (eds) (1991) Classroom concordancing. *English Language Research Journal, 4*. Birmingham: Birmingham University.

Jones, R. (1997) Creating and using a corpus of spoken German. In A. Wichmann, S. Fligelstone, T. McEnery and G. Knowles (eds) *Teaching and Language Corpora* 146–56. London/New York: Longman.

Kennedy, G. (1998) *An Introduction to Corpus Linguistics*. New York: Longman.

Lutzeier, P. (1998) *German Studies. Old and new challenges*. Bern: Peter Lang.

McEnery, T. and Wilson, A. (2001) *Corpus Linguistics*. Edinburgh: Edinburgh University Press.

Möllering, M. (2001) Teaching German modal particles. A corpus-based approach. *Language Learning & Technology* 5 (3): 130–51.

Roche, J. (2000) *Reading German. A multi-media self-study course on reading German for professional and technical purposes. Vol 1. Introduction.* Toronto: Canadian Scholar's Press Inc.

Rogalla, H. and Rogalla, W. (1985) *German for Academic Purposes. An introduction to reading academic publications*. Berlin/München: Langenscheidt.

Scott, M. and Johns, T. (1993) *MicroConcord*. Oxford: Oxford University Press.

Sinclair, J. (1991) *Corpus, Concordance, Collocation*. Oxford: Oxford University Press.

Svartvik, J. (ed.) (1992) *Directions in Corpus Linguistics*. Berlin: Mouton de Gruyter.

Thomas, J. and Short, M. (1996) *Using Corpora for Language Research*. London: Longman.

Thurstun, J. and Candlin, C. N. (1997) *Exploring Academic English*: *a workbook for student essay writing*. Sydney: National Centre for English Language Teaching and Research.

Tribble, C. and Jones, G. (1990) *Concordances in the Classroom*. Harlow: Longman.

Wichmann, A., Fligelstone, S. McEnery, T. and Knowles, G. (eds) (1997) *Teaching and Language Corpora*. London/New York: Longman.

Wilson, A. (1996) *German Quickly. A grammar for reading German*. New York: Peter Lang.

8   Academic language development programme (widening participation)

Pascaline Scalone and Brian Street

Abstract

This paper outlines ongoing research on a widening participation programme with particular reference to academic language development. It is organised into four parts: (1) The context of the programme; (2) the theoretical framing in terms of academic literacies, and the concepts of 'activity frames'; 'genres'; and 'modes'; (3) Research Findings and (4) Focus. In the context of integrating research and practice in applied language work across Europe that is the focus of this issue of the BAAL Working Papers, the project described here will be of special interest to those working in academic literacies. A key theme is that, although the focus of the programme described here is on 'EAL' students, in practice much of what we have to say applies to students in general and will be relevant to colleagues in university departments working in a variety of language contexts in different countries. Students making the transition from school or work into university contexts encounter new discourse communities, new requirements on their academic language resource and new ways of being a student. The academic literacies perspective that we elaborate upon below offers a broader theoretical and practical approach to these transitions than the dominant 'study skills' model and when we have presented on this at European wide conferences (cf. EEAW; EAIE) there have been many points of convergence (see Jones et al., 2000).

The Academic Language Development (ALD) programme also offers some useful insights into and perhaps a critical perspective on the Content and Language Integrated Learning (CLIL) initiative, supported by the European Commission, which likewise offers support for additional language learning across Europe (http://www.clilcompendium.com/). The five dimensions listed in the CLIL Compendium, relating to culture, environment, language, content and learning, could be taken as a basis for also analysing the ALD programme described here. For instance, the concepts of 'academic literacies' and of 'genre and mode switching' described below could be usefully linked to each of these features. However, the experience of ALD programme to date suggests that it is less directive than the CLIL initiative, the pedagogy is more interactive and the research more ethnographic in style. Such comparisons might provide a fruitful basis for further research that locates the ALD programme in the larger context of European initiatives at the same time as subjecting those initiatives to the comparative rigour of the kinds of case studies we describe here.

1   The context of the programme within UK higher education policy

This programme was designed to provide a non-credit bearing English language Development course for 'A' level (Year 12) students from linguistic minority community backgrounds attending schools in the locality of King's College London, who would like to further their studies at university (not just at King's – a key 'widening participation' requirement was that the programme did not simply serve as a 'hidden' selection device for KCL for future students). The programme of work was intended to provide additional opportunities for dedicated 'A' level students from the local areas who were still in the process of learning English as an additional language. It was hoped that participation in the Programme would enhance both their 'A' level performance and their chances of entering higher education. Although the focus of the Programme has been on ethnic minority students in the immediate London vicinity, the methods and outcomes are likely to prove of wider significance for EAL students in England, such as those from Europe being assessed according to the European Language Passport Programme. The programme consists of three hour sessions and runs in term time on Saturday mornings, from January to December, with fewer sessions in the summer term according to the students' exam timetable. The course is not an English language course, but rather focuses on developing the use of academic English in higher educational contexts in the UK. Most of the students have not spent a lot of time in the UK, and so can be unfamiliar with the academic language and literacy practices required for university courses in this country.

2   Theoretical framings

In both the programme design and the research, we drew upon a number of key concepts that we set out briefly here before showing how we applied them to specific data: academic literacies; 'activity frames'; 'genres'; and 'modes'.

2.1   Academic literacies

One of the underpinning concepts for the ALD programme was that of 'academic literacies' (Street, 1996), derived from the research on student writing in higher education conducted by Lea and Street (1998) and since elaborated by Lea and Stierer (1997), Jones et al. (2000), Lillis (2001), Lea (2004), Lea and Street (forthcoming) etc. The ideas associated with this growing tradition of inquiry also provided a framework for generating and now for analysing the research data.

This approach addresses the ways in which student writing in higher education can be viewed in terms of three models: study skills; academic socialisation; and academic literacies. Each successively encapsulates the other so that the academic literacies model incorporates the other two whilst offering a broader perspective on the writing process. According to Lea and Street, the study skills approach assumes that literacy is a set of atomised skills which students have to learn and which are then transferable to other contexts. The focus is on attempts to 'fix' problems with student learning, which are treated as a kind of pathology. The theory of language on which this model is based emphasises surface features, grammar and spelling.

The academic socialisation perspective challenges the narrow skills approach and instead poses the task of the tutor/advisor as being to inculcate students into a new 'culture', that of the academy. The focus is on student orientation to learning and interpretation of learning tasks. Although more sensitive to both the student as learner and to the cultural context, the approach has nevertheless been criticised from Lea and Street's third perspective, the academic literacies model. For instance, the socialisation approach assumes that the academy is one 'culture', whose norms and practices have simply to be learned to provide access to the whole institution; it fails to recognise or theorise institutional practices, including processes of change and the exercise of power. These issues are particularly important when helping 'non traditional' students access the literacy practices of the academy, as in the ALD programme.

The academic literacies approach sees literacies as social practices, in the way addressed in New Literacy Studies (Street, 1984, 1995; Barton, 1994; Gee, 1991). It views student writing and learning as issues at the level of epistemology and identities rather than simply skill or socialisation. From the student point of view a dominant feature of academic literacy practices is the requirement to switch between communicative practices, including genres, fields, and disciplines, from one setting to another, and within a setting (an issue we try to bring out in the present account); to deploy a repertoire of linguistic practices appropriate to each setting; and to handle the social meanings and identities that each evokes. The emphasis on identities and social meanings draws attention to deeper affective and ideological conflicts in such switching and use of the linguistic repertoire. A student's personal identity – who am 'I' – may be challenged by the forms of writing required in different disciplines and students may feel threatened and resistant – 'this isn't me' (Lea, 1994; Ivanic, 1998). We tried to take account of these deeper issues associated with student writing both as we developed the ALD course and as we conducted the research being reported on here.

2.2   'Activity frames'

Sessions on academic literacies within the ALD programme aimed at raising students' awareness of the different uses of language in different curriculum-based practices in the context of the academy, and they were structured in terms of different types of 'activity'. Since this research aimed at understanding how students engage with academic literacies, we decided to collect the texts students interacted with as well as the ones they produced in different activities. The concept of 'activity frame' was used as a research tool, in order to identify and contextualise the different activities observed and the different texts collected. The notion of 'frame', borrowed from the field of sociology (Goffman, 1959) is useful here to help us to identify and analyse the units of interaction in the classroom in which different curriculum-oriented texts were produced by participants. In most sessions, students engaged in a range of activities, including group discussions, group production of OHPs, presentations and individual written summaries of discussions. Within these activities they were asked to interact with and produce different types of texts, such as an OHP slide, written notes and a paragraph of discursive prose. The activities differed in terms of the dynamics of text production, genres and types of representation used. Even though these activities were designed for the specific purpose of the ALD classroom, they were also meant to reflect typical activities at university.

    An activity may comprise therefore different genres. This is the reason why, the notion of frame is useful in this study to encapsulate the different texts characterised by different genres with which students have to interact. Within each frame it is possible to observe the types of academic literacies that students need in order to participate in the classroom. The next section focuses on the different genres interacting within these frames.

2.3   Genres

Drawing on the work of Kress (2003: 118–19, especially discussion of uses of the label 'genre') we defined genres as types of text, both spoken and written, such as student discussions, written notes, letters, academic essays etc. We wanted to help students be more aware of the different language – and more broadly semiotic – practices associated with different genres. Van Dijk's definition captures well the link we identify between cultural practices and different genres which he defines as:

> different ways of using language to achieve different culturally established tasks, and texts of different genres are texts which are achieving different purposes in the culture. (1997: 236)

In one of the earlier ALD course sessions, one of the tutors gave a presentation on genre switching (see Figure 8.1). He drew attention, for instance, to the fact that prior to having a discussion, just having thoughts and ideas about a subject already involves certain kinds of representation, with different entailments than required in other forms or genres. Thoughts may, for instance, be free flowing, they may not always operate in sentences and they may include images and other non linguistic semiosis such as colours. When the students were asked to move into group talk and discussion, however, they would be required to provide some explicitness, to take account of their interlocutor and to employ specific language features and defined speech patterns. This, then, we identified as a different genre. Likewise, as students shifted to taking notes, new requirements came into play, such as the need for more explicit attention to structure, use of headings, layout etc. and use of visual as well as language 'modes'. We encouraged students to make presentations to the whole class, using overhead projector slides and again these have particular genre features, such as highlighting of key terms, use of single words and layout. Finally, they were asked to provide a page of written text based upon the discussions and overheads and these required joined up sentences, attention to coherence and cohesion, use of formal conventions and attention to editing and revision. Each 'genre' then, had different qualities and we were concerned that students had not always been made explicitly aware of this in their school work as they were required to move between different genres or given time to dwell on and develop the distinctive features of each, or to address the question of their relationship, including the fluid overlap of the boundaries of each genre (see Figure 8.1).

GENRE/ MODE SWITCHING

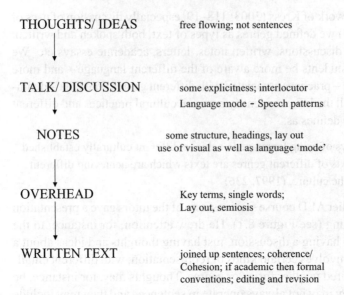

THOUGHTS/ IDEAS   free flowing; not sentences

TALK/ DISCUSSION   some explicitness; interlocutor
                         Language mode - Speech patterns

NOTES   some structure, headings, lay out
                         use of visual as well as language 'mode'

OVERHEAD   Key terms, single words;
                         Lay out, semiosis

WRITTEN TEXT   joined up sentences; coherence/
                         Cohesion; if academic then formal
                         conventions; editing and revision

QUESTION: How do genres/ modes vary across disciplines/ subjects/ fields?

GENRE: type of text e.g. formal/ informal e.g. notes/ letters/ academic essay
MODE: 'a regularised organised set of resources for meaning-making'
    e.g. image, gaze, gesture, movement, music, speech, writing
DISCIPLINE: field of study, academic subject
    e.g. geography, chemistry; Business Studies; Area Studies
SWITCHING/ TRANSFORMATION: changing meanings and representations
from one mode (e.g. speech) into another mode (e.g. writing); often involves
just a different 'mix' of both modes e.g. writing/ layout

Figure 8.1: Genre/mode switching

We asked, for instance, how do genres and modes vary across disciplines, subjects and fields? Students from science disciplines appeared less familiar with extended prose but adept at structured layout and use of signs, whilst social science students had had more written work to do in their school practice but had not necessarily differentiated its features from those of talk and visual layout as explicitly as we were doing in these sessions. In some cases they reported that teachers would follow a discussion by asking them to 'write it up' without necessarily making explicit the different requirements as they switched genre. A basic premise of our pedagogy in the course was that in learning how to engage in academic discourse, students need explicit attention to such switching, to the transformations and changing meanings and representations as they switch from one genre to another. Likewise, we drew attention to the way such switches often involve a different 'mix' of two or more genres, such as the notion that writing always creates meaning through layout as well as the use of words. From a research perspective, we used the concept of genre as both a key focus for observation and analysis as we recorded classroom interactions and as a key question in our formulation of research aims – 'how far was genre a focus of classroom activity and what meanings were attached to it by the participants?'

2.4   Modes

As we focused on the different genres that participants used within and across different activity frames, the issue of representation also needed to be addressed. Multisemiotic theories of communication emphasise the need to look at all forms of communication in terms of their representation deploying different modes: linguistic, actional and visual (Kress & van Leeuwen, 1996). When we analysed the data collected, a multimodal analysis enabled us to depict the range of meanings expressed in the different activity frames. It also allowed us to identify the types of multimodal literacies that students needed. We will discuss the relations between genres and modes in more detail through the data analysis in the following sections.

3   Research aims and preliminary findings: genres and academic literacies in the ALD programme

Research aims

In the ALD programme, members of the team both taught and engaged in ethnographic-style research. The aim of the research was to provide a data base from which future inquiries could be conducted and to make some preliminary interpretations as to how the programme was working. The focus was on actual classroom activities and on students' views on the ALD programme. One of the teachers, who was also a member of the research team observed that the ALD programme:

tries to challenge some of the expectations students may have met at school
... about language as narrowly defined ... the course involves issues of
discourse, genre, writing as social process ... within a notion of building on
what they already had and bring to the programme rather than treating them
as a deficit and just fixing that.

The research aims mentioned above, led us to explore how and whether such
teaching objectives were being met. We will show some of the data, in the
light of theoretical framings outlined above and we will draw out some initial
interpretations.

Throughout the data analysis process, we attempted to develop a triangular
interaction between students, teachers and researchers. We made use of various
tools for data collection such as video and audio recordings, a research diary
and portfolio. The diary contained general field notes, particular contextual
observations, a range of comments from participants, and researcher's questions for analysis. The portfolio comprised materials distributed by teachers
and materials produced by students such as small essays, text summaries,
OHPs for presentations, notes, and personal statements. The data collected so
far include: naturally occurring video and audio classroom data; video- and
audio-taped interviews with teachers and students; and work samples produced
by students.

The data from these particular sessions consist of: contextual information
about sessions and particular activities, extracts from group interactions during
these activities, a range of texts produced, and additional information from
students and teachers interviews.

3.2   Researching multimodal aspects of academic literacies

Teachers encouraged students to use different modes of communication to
express different types of meaning such as for instance mind-maps to organise
different levels of content (see Figures 8.2, 8.3 and 8.4 in appendix). The
teacher also illustrated throughout the sessions the communicative potentials
of various semiotic resources and the fact that different genres are characterised
by different configurations and combinations of modes of communication.

Teachers in the programme attempted to raise students' awareness of the
issues of genre control and the multiple nature of literacy. For instance, they
encouraged students to shape their notes in mind-maps, and also to use gesture,
tone, body-posture and gaze during presentations. In the example below, a
teacher is giving some feedback to students after their OHP presentations.

1 T: You did a very useful thing (.) occasionally looking at your notes (..)
2   just as a reminder (…) I can't remember all the points (…) so just a
3   couple of headings remember to look at the audience and not at your
4   notes (.) to establish some eye-contact (…) instead of looking at your
5   shoes so watch your posture (..) and also it is very important to speak in a
6   loud (.) clear voice (.) as some people at the back may not hear you (.)

Many of the students were not familiar yet with the discursive practices of the academy and this required that students and teachers had to collaboratively construct a range of content-based meanings. This collaborative construction of meaning operated through what we could label a 'metalanguage' across these different activities, as teachers attempted to raise students' awareness of the different genres of activities and the range of semiotic resources that they needed to exploit in order to represent a range of content-based meanings.

This metalanguage can be identified in a session in which students were asked to take notes during a lecture on the concept of 'genre'. By having the opportunity to compare and discuss their notes in groups with a tutor, students were able to evaluate the notes taken in terms of their usefulness to represent, structure and categorise different types and levels of content:

13 T: yes but how do things link together (?) to write a good essay (?) how do
14   things relate
15 K: I have not planned for it (.) but any ideas change and the plan changes
16   along (.) if too strictly focused then no space for creative writing (…)
17 [T: you do a plan write it revise it re-plan write revise (.) in terms of plan
18   structure we have 3 models here (*referring to map*)]

During this discussion the teacher referred to some key concepts related to the structure of information such as 'formal, informal, register, genre, linear, structured map, layers, levels, and links' and which he illustrated through the mind-map he produced (see Figures 8.2–8.3 in appendix). In this context, however, the students employ literacy practices with which they are familiar and which may be at odds with the ones they are being encouraged to engage with. Karim, for instance, produces a mind map that in fact looks like linear prose (Figure 8.4 in appendix). However, in the context of the ALD programme, he was also able to engage in a discussion of this contested practice and of the relations between multimodal representations and academic literacies. He defended his model of note-taking, which was more linear, as more productive for organising his thinking and leaving spacing to make creative changes:

6 K: put things together (.) linear presentation is clear (?)
7 T: you need to develop it in a more structured map
8 K: first notes help you to remember not the whole lecture but the structure

9   of it and from the structure you remember more information
10 T: different layers need to appear as genre etc…
11 K: what you ask is too much (.) it takes too much time (.) better keeping it
12   to the structure

Such concepts and discussions facilitated the structuring of ideas for academic
writing which many students reported to have benefited from.

3.3   Hybrid genres and multimodal representations

Throughout the course students were invited to reflect on the different genres
they are exposed to at school and in the ALD programme, the way these genres
sometimes interact and differ. Some genres interacted in the sense that students
evaluated some of the activity frames and their corresponding genres on the
basis of school experience. However, the genres that need to be mastered at
university level differ in subtle ways. In mastering these new genres students
interacted with the demands of the academy, and at the level of communication
this resulted in the creation of hybrid genres. Hybrid genres are created out of
features from different genres belonging to their repertoires and from the various academic genres they were exposed to in the ALD programme. Mastering
these hybrid genres allowed them to participate in the different activity frames
in the course, while expressing their own personal styles.

Some students, for instance, conveyed their personal styles through draw-
ings which they added on their OHPs, where some data is visually represented
next to the linguistic data as forms of illustration. At the top right of the page
in Figure 8.2 (see appendix) a fat man is drawn next to 'less active, boredom,
overeating' and at the bottom of the page a coffin and a cemetery are represented
below 'THEN U DIE' written in capital letters which seems to enhance the
dramatic effect of this statement.

The students expressed through their use of particular genres and modes
the strategies that they favoured over the ones suggested in the course. This
was exemplified during the group discussion on the potential of mind-maps
for essay structuring.

By expressing personal styles and learning strategies during classroom
activities and engaging with their related genres, students participated both in
the community of the academy and in the community formed by the students
during the course. Furthermore, by engaging with the types of academic literacies required in higher education in this country, they collaboratively interacted
with official requirements and participated in learning-oriented activities.

4   Preliminary conclusions

This paper aimed to identify different issues associated with the learning of new academic literacies. In the ALD classroom, different genres operated across different combinations of modes throughout the dynamics of activities. The data suggest that students did not always perceive the dynamics of communication in the classroom which operated at the level of genre (e.g. switching from making an summary to discussing the article, or from producing an OHP to presenting it to the rest of the classroom etc.), and at the level of mode (switching between the written mode and the spoken and actional mode, or from the visual mode to the spoken, visual and actional etc.). In the analysis of the ways in which students recognised and interacted with classroom practices, the issues of activity frames, genres and representations needed to be brought to their attention and addressed together as they are inherently linked. This constructive dimension of the ALD pedagogy, then, was reflected through the collaborative activities as teachers aimed to promote genre control and awareness of the hybrid nature of academic literacies: mixing and switching between different genres and modes. Moreover, the pedagogy left a space for combining/mixing students' cultural-capital curriculum and institutional requirements. Through the genre of discussion, for instance, students had the opportunity to engage with higher education practices and reflect on how these interacted with their own school practices in London and back home. As mentioned at the outset, we might fruitfully ask how all of this relates to the CLIL dimensions, noting for instance the interrelated features of culture, environment, language, content and learning that are evident in these practices. Treating the student learning experience as rooted in cultural knowledge and specific to the environment – in this case that of higher education in the UK but also potentially providing a constructive way of addressing the implications of CLIL in practice – moves us away from a narrow 'skills' based approach that would treat academic language as somehow generic and the same across environments and cultures. In the ALD programme it is apparent that the 'focus points' are realised differently in this sociolinguistic environment and for this age-range of learners, than they would be in other environments and for other learners. The implications of this for access to universities may be considerable not only in the UK but across Europe. In contemporary conditions, university and higher education students are expected, indeed required to engage in multiple forms of learning including with rapidly changing technologies. Treating such students as collaborators in the development of the academic literacies necessary for engagement with such practices and technologies in the sphere of higher education, can perhaps offer a different and more supportive route to 'widening participation' than the more traditional focus on either study skills or academic socialisation. How far this can actually be realised in practice requires more research; this report represents a first step in that direction (cf. also Leung & Safford, 2004; Lea & Street, forthcoming).

References

Barton, D. (1994) *Literacy: an introduction to the ecology of written language*. London: Blackwell.

Bazerman, C. (1988) *Shaping Written Knowledge: the genre and activity of the experimental article in science*. Madison, Wisconsin: University of Wisconsin Press.

Berkenkotter, C. and Huckin, T. (1995) *Genre Knowledge in Disciplinary Communication*. New York: Lawrence Erlbaum and Assocs.

Creme, P. and Lea, M. (1997) *Writing at University: a guide for students*. Milton Keynes: Open University Press.

Gee, J. (1991) *Social Linguistics and Literacies: ideology in discourses*. Brighton: Falmer Press.

Goffman, E. (1959) *The Presentation of Self in Everyday Life*. New York: Doubleday.

Green, J. and Bloome, D. (1997) Ethnography and ethnographers of and in education: a situated perspective. In J. Flood, S. Heath and D. Lapp (eds) *A Handbook of Research on Teaching Literacy through the Communicative and Visual Arts* 181–202. New York: Simon and Shuster Macmillan.

Ivanic, R. (1998) *Writing and Identity: the discoursal construction of identity in academic writing*. Amsterdam: John Benjamins.

Jones, C., Turner, J. and Street, B. (2000) *Student Writing in Higher Education: theory and practice*. Amsterdam: John Benjamins.

Kress, G. (2003) *Literacy in the New Media Age*. London: Routledge.

Kress, G. and van Leeuwen, T. (1996) *Reading Images: the grammar of visual design*. London: Routledge.

Lea, M. (1994) I thought I could write till I came here: student writing in higher education. In G. Gibbs (ed.) *Improving Student Learning: theory and practice*. Oxford: OSCD.

Lea, M. (2004) Academic literacies: a pedagogy for course design. *Studies in Higher Education* 29(6): 739–56.

Lea, M. and Street, B. (1997) Student writing and faculty feedback in higher education: an academic literacies approach. *Studies in Higher Education* 23(2): 157–72.

Lea, M. and Street, B. (1999) Writing as academic literacies: understanding textual practices in higher education. In C. Candlin and K. Hyland (eds) *Writing Texts, Processes and Practices* 62–81. London: Longman.

Lea, M. and Street, B. (forthcoming) Revisiting 'academic literacies'; two case studies from the UK. *Theory into Practice* (Special edition) *Literacies of and for a Diverse Society*.

Lea, M. and Stierer, B. (2000) *Student Writing in Higher Education*: *new contexts*. Buckingham: Open University Press.

Leung, C. and Safford, K. (2005) Non-traditional students in higher education in the United Kingdom: English as an additional language and literacies. In B. Street (ed.) *Literacies Across Educational Contexts*: *mediating learning and teaching*. Philadelphia: Caslon Publishing.

Lillis, T. (2001) *Student Writing*: *access, regulation, desire*. London: Routledge.

Russell, D. (1991) *Writing in the Academic Disciplines, 1870–1990*: *a curricular history*. Carbondale: S. Illinois University Press.

Street, B. (1984) *Literacy in Theory and Practice*. Cambridge: Cambridge University Press.

Street, B. (1995) *Social Literacies*. London: Longman.

Street, B. (1996) Academic Literacies. In D. Baker, J. Clay and C. Fox (eds) *Alternative Ways of Knowing*: *literacies, numeracies, sciences* 101–34. London: Falmer Press.

Taylor, G., Ballard, B., Beasley, V., Hanne, B., Clanchy, J. and Nightingale, P. (1988) *Literacy By Degrees*. *Society for Research in Higher Education*. Milton Keynes: Open University.

Van Djik, T. (ed.) (1997) *Discourse as Structure and Process*. London: Sage.

Appendix

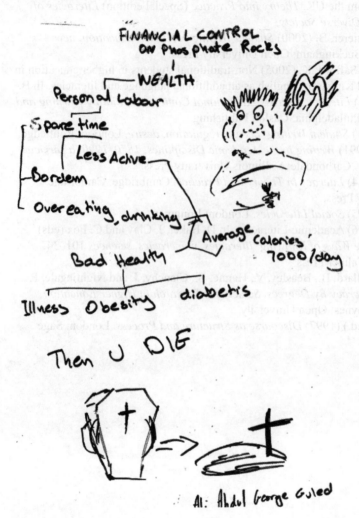

FINANCIAL CONTROL
ON Phosphate Rocks
|
WEALTH
Personal Labour
Spare time
Less Active
Boredom
Overeating, drinking
Average Calories 7000/day
Bad Health
Illness   Obesity   diabetis

Then U DIE

AI: Abdul George Guled

Figure 8.2: Students' OHPs

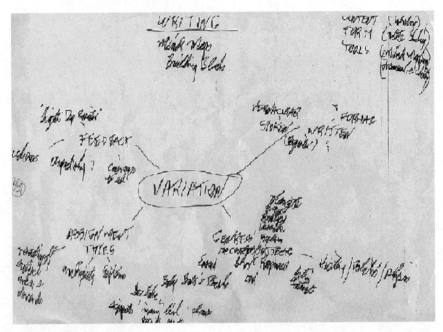

Figure 8.3: Teacher's mind-map

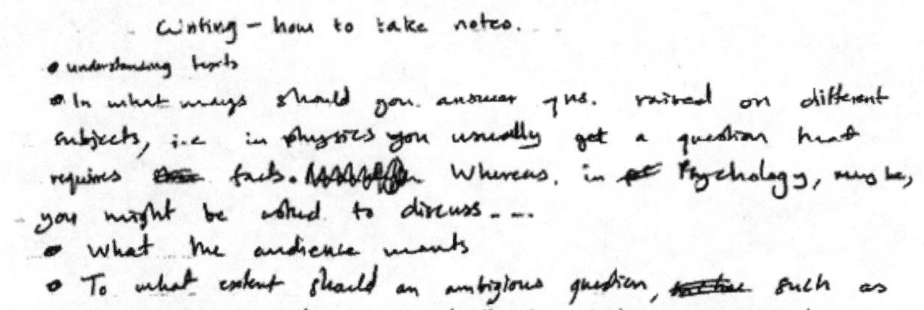

Figure 8.4: Student's mind-map

9   Evaluating Europe: parameters of evaluation in the British press

Monika Bednarek

Abstract

This paper deals with the linguistic expression of speaker/writer opinion – a phenomenon variously known as evaluation, stance and appraisal. It identifies certain semantic dimensions – evaluative parameters – along which evaluations can proceed and analyses some of their linguistic manifestations in a 500,000-word corpus of British (broadsheet and tabloid) newspaper discourse on the European Constitution. Examples of such evaluative parameters are the parameter of EMOTIVITY (the expression of approval or disapproval), COMPREHENSIBILITY (concerning the extent to which aspects of the world are evaluated as more or less comprehensible on the part of the writer), EVIDENTIALITY (evaluations concerning the source of a proposition), STYLE (evaluative comments on the communication itself) and IMPORTANCE (concerning the significance of what is evaluated). The analysis of evaluative parameters is supplemented with a traditional collocational study of keywords in the corpus. The results show some of the key sites and characteristics of evaluation concerning the European Constitution in the corpus, in particular the differences between the broadsheets and the tabloids.

Introduction

In our ever faster changing environment and with the advances of new information technologies, the media have become increasingly powerful. But despite the growing relevance of European issues that transcend national boundaries, there is no pan-European media publication which has as much influence as the national newspapers of its member countries. These national publications in turn influence individual readers' views by covering stories with a particular slant.[1] Applied linguistics can use its methodology to uncover this process of 'recontextualisation' (Caldas-Coulthard, 2003: 273) and thus perhaps contribute to 'reconfiguring Europe' (for studies on attitudes towards Europe see also Musolff et al., 1996; Convery et al., 1997; Mautner, 2000; Florack & Piontkowski, 2000 and Good et al., 2001).

In this paper I will analyse parameters of evaluation in British newspaper discourse covering issues revolving around the European constitution. Evaluation, or the expression of speaker opinion, has only recently become the focus of linguistic analysis and this mainly within studies of EAP (English for Academic Purposes) (Bondi & Mauranen, 2003) or – under the name of *appraisal* – within SFL (Systemic Functional Linguistics) (Martin, 2000; White, 2002; Macken-Horarik & Martin, 2003; Coffin & O'Halloran, 2004; Martin & White, 2005).

In contrast, the approach taken here is eclectic, drawing on a wide range of linguistic studies on evaluation to establish its own framework of evaluative parameters, which is then applied to the analysis of a 500,000-word corpus of British 'tabloids' and 'broadsheets'. In the following paragraphs I shall first provide a short introduction to my parameter-based framework of evaluation before presenting the results of the application of this framework to a specialised corpus of newspaper discourse.

The parameter-based framework of evaluation

A parameter-based approach to the expression of speaker opinion takes as a springboard for the analysis of evaluation Thompson and Hunston's (2000) definition of *evaluation* as:

> the broad cover term for the expression of the speaker's or writer's attitude or stance towards, viewpoint on, or feelings about the entities or propositions that he or she is talking about. That attitude may relate to certainty or obligation or desirability or any of a number of other sets of values. (Thompson & Hunston, 2000: 5)[2]

Evaluation in this sense has many similarities with the notions of *stance* and *appraisal* (see above). Adopting a parameter-based approach to evaluation means that these 'sets of values' are identified as *evaluative parameters* (a term taken up from Francis, 1995). It is assumed that there are certain parameters along which speakers can evaluate aspects of the world, and that each of the proposed parameters involves a different semantic dimension along which the evaluation can proceed, covering evaluations of aspects of the world as

- good-bad (the parameter of EMOTIVITY)[3]
- important-unimportant (the parameter of IMPORTANCE)
- expected-unexpected (the parameter of EXPECTEDNESS)

Appraisal	Francis (1995)	Thompson & Hunston (2000)	Conrad & Biber (2000)	Biber and Finegan (1988)	Lemke (1998)	Parameter-based framework
Attitude		positive – negative parameter	attitudinal stance	*amazingly* adverbials: expressing attitudes towards the content independent of its epistemological status	desirability / inclination	EMOTIVITY
• Affect	rationality					
• Judgement	value / appropriacy					(MENTAL STATE)
• Appreciation						
	predictability	expectedness / obviousness	epistemic stance	*actually* adverbials: expressing actuality, emphasis, greater certainty / truth than expected	usuality / expectability	EXPECTEDNESS
	obviousness				comprehensibility / obviousness	COMPREHENSIBILITY
				maybe adverbials: expressing possibility, likelihood, questionable assertions, hedging		EVIDENTIALITY
Engagement	truth	certainty			warrantability / probability	RELIABILITY
	modality			*surely* adverbials: expressing conviction or certainty		
	importance	relevance / importance	style stance		importance / significance	IMPORTANCE
				honestly adverbials: expressing manner of speaking		STYLE
				generally adverbials: expressing approximation, generalisation	normativity / appropriateness	POSSIBILITY / NECESSITY
	ability				humorousness / seriousness	SERIOUSNESS
Graduation					—	

Table 9.1: The parameter-based framework of evaluation[4]

- comprehensible-incomprehensible (the parameter of COMPREHENSI-BILITY)
- serious-funny (the parameter of SERIOUSNESS)
- (not)possible-(not)necessary (the parameter of POSSIBILITY / NECESSITY)
- genuine-fake (the parameter of RELIABILITY)

Evaluative parameters are also concerned with evaluations of propositions as being more or less reliable (RELIABILITY: LOW/MEDIAN/HIGH), evaluations of the language that is used (the parameter of STYLE), of other social actors' mental states (the parameter of MENTAL STATE), and of the source of the speaker's knowledge (the parameter of EVIDENTIALITY). The parameter-based framework to evaluation is elaborated and synthesised from previous research, and in particular owes much to Lemke (1998) (compare Table 9.1).

These evaluative parameters can also be combined in that, for instance, expressions such as *seem* and *appear* are regarded as evaluations of both EVIDENTIALITY and RELIABILITY. In the Longman grammar these verbs are described as 'characteri[sing] the subject predicative as a **perception** that is not necessarily accurate' (Biber et al., 1999: 447, my emphasis), and as having a 'probability meaning' (Biber et al., 1999: 693), hence expressing at the same time EVIDENTIALITY (perception) and RELIABILITY (probability). Similarly, reporting expressions (e.g. *claim that*, *promise that*) can be considered as evaluations of EVIDENTIALITY and STYLE, indicating that what follows is based on hearsay, and simultaneously commenting on the illocutionary act involved.[5]

Evaluating Europe – the results

The above-mentioned framework of evaluation can – like *appraisal* – be used for a detailed manual analysis of individual texts, providing information on any underlying ideology. However, – like *stance* (cf. Biber & Finegan, 1989; Biber et al., 1999; Conrad & Biber, 2000) – it can also be employed in corpus-based analyses, as is the case here (using Wordsmith Tools; Scott, 1999).

The empirical basis for this analysis was a 500,000-word corpus of newspaper texts, consisting of 498 broadsheet texts (375,394 words from *The Daily/Sunday Telegraph*, *The Guardian*, *The Independent/Independent on Sunday*, and *The Times/Sunday Times*) and 234 tabloid texts (123,153 words from *The Express*, *The Daily Mail/Mail on Sunday*, *The Daily Mirror/The Sunday Mirror*, *The Daily Star/Sunday Star*, and *The Sun*), featuring the search expression *European Constitution*. The corpus (which will be referred to as *European Constitution Corpus*, or ECC, from now on) covers a period of six months (5 November 2003 to 5 May 2004) and contains mixed news categories (features, hard news, comment etc.). The smaller size of the tabloid corpus results from the fact that Europe as a 'newsworthy' topic plays a much less significant role in the tabloids than in the broadsheets.[6]

For practical reasons not all of the evaluative parameters were examined in the ECC. Instead, the focus was on some of the most significant or most frequent linguistic devices of evaluation (evaluators) of the parameters of EMOTIVITY, COMPREHENSIBILITY, EVIDENTIALITY/STYLE, and IMPORTANCE in the corpus as identified in a previous study of news reportage. In this study (see also Bednarek, 2006) a 70,000 word corpus of newspaper discourse was analysed manually for **all** linguistic expressions of evaluation. Those devices that were found to be most significant or most frequent in this study were the basis for choosing the linguistic expressions analysed in the ECC.[7]

EMOTIVITY

Concerning the parameter of EMOTIVITY the focus was on the evaluators *fail/failure* and *succeed/success*, since they are identified as 'very clearly evaluative' by Thompson and Hunston (2000: 14).

In the tabloid sub-corpus there are three main topics concerning Europe and failure: the failure of EU members to agree, the failure of EU talks or negotiations, and the failure of Europe/the EU Constitution. In the bigger broadsheet sub-corpus *fail/failure* is also associated with these topics, and is additionally used for conditional statements asking what would happen if countries (mostly Britain) fail to endorse the constitution as well as for predictions that a referendum would fail. Here are some examples:

(1)   The shambolic **failure** of **negotiations** has left Mr Blair's European strategy in tatters. (tb)

(2)   WARNING: **EU DRAFT** SET TO **FAIL** (tb)

(3)   In practice, this hands power to the elitist, undemocratic bureaucracy of **Brussels**, presided over by **failed** politicians nominated by their cronies. (bs)

(4)   perhaps the most critical section is Article 14, which gives the EU the power to 'ensure co-ordination' of economic and social policies, thereby entrenching **Europe's failed** economic model. (bs)

(5)   **The EU is failing** to face up to the realities of the 21st century. The communications revolution means that individuals now have a global reach and a global outlook. (bs)

(6)   What happens **if** it [constitution] **fails** to come into effect? (bs)

(7)   Unless Iraq comes round, Blair's credit may not be enough to get him
       through a referendum, and a **failed referendum** in Britain could have large
       consequences (bs)

As becomes apparent from these examples, there is at times a huge difference
in the evaluative potential of *fail/failure*. It seems to range from more to less
evaluative, shading at times into mere negation. However, it might be argued
that there is a persistent association of Europe/the European Constitution with
failure, which leaves its impression on the readers: in Hoey's (2004) terms,
they are 'primed' to expect failure when coming across certain Europe-related
topics.

If we compare the supposed positive counterpart to *fail/failure*, namely
succeed/success – which might be expected to express positive evaluation
towards Europe – a similar observation of a graded evaluative force can be
made. Furthermore, the evaluators are by no means positive in their every
usage. In fact, almost all of the (few) relevant occurrences in the tabloids
are negative:

(8)   So he set up a new political party with the single aim of **forcing**
       Conservative and Labour to commit to a referendum before taking
       Britain into the eurozone. It was a tremendous **success.** (tb)

(9)   Given that **a main qualification for success in Brussels has to be an**
       understanding of corruption, dishonesty, freeloading and graft, Mr
       Mandelson would clearly go there with several massive advantages over any
       potential rivals. (tb)

(10)   I wish she [the Queen] would object to **the slowmotion putsch against our**
       liberties that will soon have achieved total success. Yet, in a dismal and
       shameful circular now being sent out by Buckingham Palace, she refuses to
       act against the new European Constitution which will reduce her Coronation
       Oath to nonsense. (tb)

None of these examples are concerned with a positive evaluation of Europe.
In Example (8), a somewhat anti-European strategy is evaluated as successful (positive), indicating a negative stance towards Europe. Example (9) is
very clearly negative towards the politicians working in Brussels and Peter
Mandelson, as seen by the explicitly negative lexical expressions *corruption*,
dishonesty, *freeloading* and *graft*. Example (10) is a very good example for
showing how writers can evaluate something as being a *success* while at the
same time expressing negative evaluation: here it is the Queen as well as the
new European Constitution that are negatively evaluated.

In the broadsheets, *success/succeed* is associated with four topics:

Anti-Europe success or negative evaluation of Europe:

(11)   The key to being **successful is adaptation** to your environment. I believe that the new draft constitution would **prevent Britain and the European Union adapting** to the great challenges we face in the 21st century …

(12)   The European Commission – the full-time bureaucrats – had two members on the Convention. They were dedicated to obtaining more influence for the commission, and they **succeeded**. […] **It is hardly an advance for democracy** when the least democratic institution in the EU is given more powers in this way

Non-factual success:

(13)   Do we wish to throw ourselves wholeheartedly into the Community, or stand on the sidelines forever making up our minds **whether we want to see it succeed or not**?

Success of the Eurosceptics:

(14)   Downing Street's private polling shows how **successful** the Eurosceptic **disinformation campaign** has been. A majority of people think signing the new European constitution would require Britain to join the EU

Success of Europe/the referendum (least frequent):

(15)   Britain's economic relationship with the continent has been a huge and vital **success** for the past 30 years, and must continue to be so.

Again, the evaluative potential of *success/succeed* clearly depends on its context and usage: it is certainly not very evaluative in non-factual usages, can be used more or less neutrally, positively (in that something is positively evaluated as a success) and negatively (in that a success is negatively evaluated). In sum, it can be argued that *fail/failure* and *success/succeed* should not be considered as 'very clearly evaluative' in all their contexts, but that in the ECC Europe/the European Constitution are in general associated with failure rather than with success.

COMPREHENSIBILITY

Regarding the parameter of COMPREHENSIBILITY I looked for the frequent evaluators *unclear/not clear*. Although there are no occurrences of these evaluators in
the tabloid sub-corpus, five of the nine occurrences in the broadsheet sub-corpus
are negative. Compare the following examples:

(16)   Mr Blair is expected to fly to Spain later today and is likely to meet Jose
        Maria Aznar, the outgoing Prime Minister. It was **unclear** last night whether
        he would be having official talks with Jose Luis Rodriguez Zapatero, the
        new Prime Minister, who was an outspoken critic of the Iraq war, but Mr
        Blair is believed to be anxious to build a relationship with him. (bs)

(17)   According to the British understanding, this post [deputy president of
        EC] will become a force for liberalising and deregulation; the French
        understanding remained **unclear.** (bs)

(18)   Much of the constitution is in the same language, more dead than either
        Latin or ancient Greek, which not only fails to enthuse its defenders but
        renders its meaning **unclear**. (bs)

(19)   On one occasion a redraft of articles dealing with defence mysteriously
        arrived just before midnight. They were written in French and the authorship
        was **unclear**. (bs)

In Example (16) *unclear* is used more or less neutrally, describing the author's
insufficient knowledge of a future state of affairs, whereas in the remaining
examples *unclear* seems to express negative evaluation. In Example (17), the
British understanding – which is implicitly evaluated positively (*liberalising*
and *deregulation* must be regarded as positively loaded here) – is contrasted
with a French understanding described as *unclear*. On the one hand, this contrast implies that the French do not share this (positive) British understanding,
on the other, it indicates that the French are not capable to put across their
views. In Example (18), the negative lexical expressions (*dead, fails to*) and
the comparison expressed by not *only ... but* work together to evaluate the
constitution as negative, as written in a 'dead' and 'incomprehensible' language, not being capable even of enthusing its proponents. The final example
is particularly interesting since there is an accumulation of evaluations of
incomprehensibility: the redraft is described as *mysteriously* arriving *just before
midnight*, with *unclear* authorship. Both *mysteriously* and *unclear* are direct
evaluators of incomprehensibility, whereas *just before midnight* seems to evoke
the context of crime and mystery. Additionally, there is a cultural assumption
that authors do not disclaim authorship unless there is something 'fishy' about

their writings. Thus, most evaluations of COMPREHENSIBILITY in the ECC are actually used to express an additional negative evaluation. Lemke (1998) calls this 'prosodic overlap' noting that:

> [t]here are many [...] cases in which we fairly liberally substitute one kind of evaluation for another, when the context makes clear which one we are really getting at. But this simple metaphoric [used in Halliday's 1994 sense] process [...] becomes in practice quite complicated as we examine how prosodic overlap between different evaluative themes in a text facilitates the shifting and overlaying of different evaluative meanings. (Lemke, 1998: 48)

Cases of such 'overlap' might be regarded as less explicit than cases where the evaluation is directly encoded. Perhaps this explains why there are no occurrences of *unclear* in the tabloid sub-corpus, though more research would be needed to support this hypothesis.

EVIDENTIALITY/STYLE

Turning now to evaluations of EVIDENTIALITY/STYLE let us look at the occurrences of *admit* in the ECC. Evaluations of EVIDENTIALITY/STYLE in general concern mostly reporting expressions which can be regarded as signalling both evaluations concerning the source of a proposition (as hearsay) and evaluative comments on the communication itself (style). These are naturally very frequent in newspaper discourse, since news is always 'embedded talk' (Bell, 1991: 52). *Admit* is a particularly interesting evaluator of EVIDENTIAL-ITY/STYLE in that it seems to additionally express the parameters of EMOTIVITY and RELIABILITY. It shows that a statement was produced reluctantly (Clayman, 1990: 87), carries the implied assumption that some negative act has been committed (Hardt-Mautner, 1995: 13) or suggests that the content of the reported proposition is negative. It is also part of Thompson's group of verbs that imply the writer's belief in the truth of the attributed proposition (Thompson, 1994: 50). Consequently, *admit* can in fact be regarded as expressing four parameters of evaluation:

- it names illocutionary acts (STYLE: ILLOCUTIONARY) and evaluates a proposition as based on hearsay (EVIDENTIALITY: HEARSAY);
- it expresses the writer's negative evaluation of the Sayer (EMOTIVITY: NEGATIVE);
- it expresses the writer's belief that what the Sayer says is true (RELIABILITY: HIGH).

This makes it an especially polyfunctional evaluator of EVIDENTIALITY/STYLE and hence a worthy object of investigation. Two aspects are particularly interesting concerning the analysis of *admit* in the corpus: the Sayers that are described as 'admitting' something, and the proposition that is said to be 'admitted'. In the tabloids, most of the Sayers are either Tony Blair himself or related to him (his ministers, his spokesman, the government etc.) – in only one instance is *admit* used in connection with Michael Howard (leader of the Conservative Party). *Admit* is thus primarily employed to criticise the government. Nevertheless, there are Sayers who are specifically Europe-related; these concern European leaders or pro-Europeans:

- *Pro-Europeans within Government*
- *the architect of the proposed reforms* [Valery Giscard d'Estaing]
- *feuding EU leaders*
- *The* [European] *Commission*
- *French Foreign Minister Dominique de Villepin*
- *the Irish leader*

Looking at the propositions that are 'admitted' in the tabloids there are a number of cases where the content of the proposition is clearly negative towards Europe or implies the 'non-necessity' of (Britain's adopting) the Constitution:

- *it* [the constitution] *is very much more than that* [a 'tidying-up exercise'] *and could even become the foundation stone for a federal superstate.*
- *BRITAIN would not be forced to leave the EU if it voted to reject the constitution*
- *the EU could carry on without it* [a constitution]
- *the Brussels superstate summit was close to collapse*
- *its* [the EC's] *hard-line tactics will be seen as 'destructive' but has vowed to press ahead with them anyway.*
- *the Eurofighter, 10 years behind schedule, billions over budget and superfluous to defence requirements in the post-Cold War age, is experiencing 'altitude problems'*

In such cases the attribution is a very clever device of allowing writers to evaluate while seeming to attribute. The Sayers to whom the evaluation is attributed are additionally negatively evaluated (as *admitting* something).

In the broadsheets sub-corpus the Sayers are more varied (in that both the government and the opposition are represented), but nevertheless no anti-Europeans occur as Sayers. The Europe-related Sayers are:

- *Jean-Pierre Raffarin, M Chirac's Prime Minister*
- *Poland*
- *strong pro-Europeans*
- *one enthusiast*
- *the summit president*
- *the Polish Government*
- *Europe's leaders*
- *He* [Signor Prodi]

Again, some of the propositions are particularly negative towards Europe or imply the necessity of a referendum/the 'non-necessity' of a constitution:

- *the pro-European cause has faltered*
- *that already over 50 per cent of the rules on British businesses are set in Brussels and the constitution gives the EU powers to impose even greater regulation.*
- *in 2002–03 50 per cent of its Bills had to be introduced to bring the department in line with EU regulations and likewise with 57 per cent of what is called secondary legislation.*
- *it* [Downing Street] *is willing to whittle down the veto in criminal justice, but not on 'key issues'.*
- *the constitution would 'involve the transfer of significant powers away from Westminster'.*
- *that 'we can't go on like this' and the EU needs 'radical reform'.*
- *failure*
- *the constitution would dramatically alter the EU and its structure*
- *the pooling of sovereignty enshrined in the constitution was a 'change in centuries of history'*
- *it would be impossible to pretend that the EU could not operate without the constitution*

However, a more detailed analysis of these and other attributed propositions would be necessary to gauge the effect of overall attribution in the ECC.

IMPORTANCE

The parameter of IMPORTANCE is the final evaluative parameter to be analysed here. The most frequent evaluators in news discourse are *senior*, *top*, *key*, *vital* and *crucial*, although they are not used to the same intents and purposes. *Senior* and *top* are predominantly related to the news value of 'eliteness' (Bell, 1991: 158) and evaluate the Sayers of quoted propositions as being of high importance (which often simultaneously implies the reliability of what is quoted). In contrast, *key*, *vital* and *crucial* are more varied in their usage.

If we compare the content of the propositions of Sayers that are described as *senior* or *top* in the two sub-corpora, the following picture emerges:

senior, top	Tabloid sub-corpus	Broadsheet sub-corpus
Number of occurrences	19	59
Number of occurrences involving attribution	15	43
In favour of referendum, against Constitution or EU	7	9
Against referendum	1	2
In favour of Constitution	0	4
Other	7	28

Table 9.2: Distribution of 'senior' and 'top' and attribution

As becomes apparent from this table, the contents of the attributed propositions of 'important' Sayers are predominantly 'anti-European' in both sub-corpora, although the broadsheets also allow 'pro-European' voices to hold the floor. In Bakhtin's sense, the broadsheets are thus more 'polyphonic' (Bakhtin, 1986: 151).

Let us now look at the other evaluators of importance, *key*, *vital* and *crucial*. These evaluators delineate 'vital issues'. In both corpora these are (1) relinquishing control and (2) the European constitution/the EU. Examples for (1) are:

(20)   Mr Blair is under pressure to **give up** Britain's veto over **key** decision making by elected British governments (tb)

(21)   So the Queen would **lose** her **key** power to make new treaties (tb)

(22)   The disastrous plan would mean Britain **having no say** in **crucial** decisions on foreign affairs, asylum, defence, agriculture and fisheries. (tb)

(23)   **Even if** Tony Blair **holds firm** to some of his **crucial** 'red lines' it will still represent a danger to our independence and sovereignty. (tb)

(24)   The leaders of 25 EU countries meet in Brussels to hammer out a deal on a European Constitution that will **alter for ever** the most **vital** aspects of our way of life. (tb)

(25)   It [the European Constitution] will, in other words, **hand over control** of the who, when and why of living in Britain to bureaucrats in Brussels, with our Parliament in Westminster **losing** all say over this **vital** area. (tb)

(26)   They will also use the publication to reassure voters that they do not plan to **give up** the national veto in **key** areas such as tax and foreign policy. (bs)

(27)   Downing Street is broadly happy with the text since Britain will **keep** the veto in **key** areas of taxation, foreign policy, and defence (bs)

(28)   Barely a day earlier, the **Prime Minister**, egged on by Gerhard Schroder, the German Chancellor, had **made crucial concessions** allowing for a deal on the European constitution by June. (bs)

(29)   **Vital** decisions about our future **would be taken by foreign judges** with no background in British law; no personal interest in our rights and freedoms. (bs)

Although some of these examples explicitly state that Britain has *not* given up control (or are non-factual), even then the implicit presumption is that it is the intention or consequence of the European Union/a European Constitution to transfer important areas of control from Britain to Europe – a central element of British Euro-scepticism (see also Teubert, 2001: 76 and Mautner, 2001: 11, 161).

Examples for (2) are:

(30)   Tawdry tactics in a **crucial** debate (tb)

(31)   Mr Blair promises an honest and open debate on the most **crucial** issue to face Britain in decades. (tb)

(32)   But France and Germany last night appeared ready to ambush the PM at **crucial** talks over breakfast. (tb)

(33)   This month, Ireland takes over the presidency of the EU, chairing the **vital** talks on a new European constitution. (tb)

(34)   Whatever the PM's motives, letting the people decide on such a **vital** issue would be sensible, fair and democratic (tb)

(35)   Blair must realise he can't get away with denying us the right to vote on this **vital** issue. (tb)

(36)   To oppose a plebiscite on what is inarguably a **vital** constitutional question looked increasingly shifty and dishonest. (tb)

(37)   The mild reprimand for the Foreign Secretary came as Britain was braced for fresh conflict over plans for the EU blueprint at **key** negotiations this weekend. Proposals to be tabled by the Italian presidency today are not expected to hold out the hope of progress on the UK's worries over tax harmonisation, defence and foreign affairs. (bs)

(38)   A WEEK from the **crucial** summit in Brussels at which the 25 European Union partners will try to reach agreement on a new European constitution, the Italian Prime Minister Silvio Berlusconi, president of the EU until (bs)

(39)   Yet it refuses to countenance the one means of publicly debating the **crucial** matter of our constitutional relationship with the EU. (bs)

On the one hand, such evaluations are used as a supporting argument in favour of a referendum. The argument goes something like 'the European constitution is a very important issue for the British people; therefore, they must be able to decide about it'. On the other hand, such evaluations are used to enhance the 'newsworthiness' of the reported topics (European negotiations etc.), presumably because such 'political' topics are not regarded by the creators of the news as inherently newsworthy for the majority of their readers.

Evaluation and collocation

So far we have seen how the application of a parameter-based framework of evaluation can give us a glance at some of the evaluation present in the ECC. Such an analysis can, and indeed should, be supplemented with a traditional collocational analysis of some keywords. As Sinclair points out: 'evidence concerning people's attitude to concepts and evaluation of them will mainly be found in linguistic expression, in the contexts of use of the words and phrases that express the concepts.' (Sinclair, 2004: 119).

In this paper I focus on the key expressions *European Constitution, European, Franco-German, France and Germany* and *Germany and France* (the numbers in brackets refer to the position of the collocates in the collocate list of Wordsmith Tools):

European Constitution

referendum (4), new (5), proposed (9), draft (10), sign (62)   broadsheets

new (4), referendum (5), proposed (9), sign (26), controversial (29),   tabloids
dangers (47), draft (49)

Here the occurrence of potentially negative collocates such as *controversial* and *dangers* points directly to the negative stance expressed in the tabloids. A superficially neutral collocate such as *sign* must be analysed in more detail in order to establish its evaluative potential. *Sign* as a collocate for *European Constitution* is usually used as part of a phrasal verb:

sign up to (33.3%), sign up (9.5%)	broadsheets
sign up to (34.4%), sign up (17.1%), sign away (12.2%)	tabloids

Again, the evaluative stance of the tabloid sub-corpus is signalled by the negative evaluator *sign away*, which once more relates Europe to the transfer of control.

Similarly, the collocates for *European* give us a good impression of the evaluation in the ECC (but see Mautner, 2000: 138 on the polysemy of *European*). Whereas the broadsheet collocates are mostly neutral (possible exceptions are *foreign* and *powers* which can be used negatively), the tabloid collocates are partly negative (*controversial, superstate, federal, foreign, powers*): [8]

European

constitution (3), union (6), referendum (8), new (9), foreign (75), powers (90)	broadsheets
constitution (3), new (5), referendum (6), union (9), superstate (38), controversial (63), federal (76), foreign (78), powers (97)	tabloids

Finally, if we look at the concordance lines for *Franco-German, France and Germany* and *Germany and France* we find that roughly 30% of occurrences in the broadsheets and roughly 40% in the tabloids either associate France and Germany with negative evaluation or with power (sometimes this coincides). [9] Some examples are:

```
again subservient to the diktats of the Franco-German alliance -with an i
s, the effective authority would be the Franco-German alliance. The oss
nnot be ratified; therefore the proposed Franco-German bureaucratic
d authority. They resent efforts by the Franco-German club to bully them
rket reforms in an attempt to challenge Franco-German dominance. Mr Azn
of a Europe which would really become a Franco-German empire, as Germany
o Portugal, Spain and Greece tumbled to Franco-German levels during the
mmon European ideal, as dictated by the Franco-German axis, than he has
tvote the previously all-powmembererful Franco-German axis.
```

```
cratic European superstate dominated by France and Germany. So will
r fellow member states. A Europe run by France and Germany was anathe
ence in a two-speed Europe dominated by France and Germany. Europea
n a week when the two giants of the EU, France and Germany, have persu
e in our interest to be at the mercy of France and Germany will surely
 no democratic support. The big boys of France and Germany want an ef
 that it is a Europe essentially run by France and Germany. And how de
ears wanted a Europe essentially run by France and Germany, with
 certain: it will continue to be run by France and Germany, just as it he
sons. But will they? The squealing from France and Germany exposes the y,
rope being run by and for the benefit of France and Germany.
reflects all our ideals. The big players Germany and France want to keep th
rlusconi's Italy, as a counterweight to Germany and France within the EU.
 after the shock of the decision to let Germany and France ignore the grow
```

Conclusion

A decade after the BAAL meeting in Salford in 1993 about 'language in a changing Europe' (Graddol & Thomas, 1995) Europe has changed in many ways. One important change concerns the adoption of a European Constitution on 29 October 2004, which was preceded by much debate. To analyse this debate with the help of linguistic tools was the focus of this study, in which I applied a parameter-based approach of evaluation to a corpus of newspaper discourse concerning the European Constitution. The results of the study seem to support the validity of the framework, in that it allows an analysis of bigger corpora rather than merely the manual analysis of individual texts. Furthermore, the tendencies of evaluation that were found with the help of this framework were confirmed by traditional collocational analyses.

Although the findings were not always quantified (and moreover, cannot be related to newspaper discourse about Europe as a whole), they give us a clear impression of some of the key sites of evaluation concerning the European Constitution in the ECC. However, a *complete* analysis of attitudes towards Europe in the British press would have to:

  (a) provide an analysis of *all* potential evaluators;
  (b) consider the difference between editorials, news stories and other sub-genres of newspaper discourse;
  (c) include texts about a variety of European topics;
  (d) attempt exact quantification in *all* cases.

As far as the ECC is concerned, the tendencies that were observed with the help of the evaluative framework are slightly different in the two sub-corpora.

In the view of the tabloids Europe consistently fails; it wants to take away vital powers from Britain and is a dangerous superstate 'essentially run by France and Germany'. Negative elite voices appear to hold the floor. Consequently, the tabloids seem to be part of the traditional Euro-sceptic discourse identified by Teubert (2001). In the eyes of the broadsheets Europe similarly wants to take away vital powers from Britain, and is associated with failures in many areas, though also (rarely) with success. Negative evaluation of Europe is not as explicit and as exclusive as in the tabloids: the broadsheets are thus not solely part of the Euro-sceptic discourse but more polyphonic.

It is also interesting to note that *when* tabloids and broadsheets express negative evaluation of Europe, they use the same kinds of arguments, which moreover, have been around for quite a long time in Great Britain (see Mautner, 2000: 314–15 on these and additional anti-European strategies and motifs).

Almost six months after the time period covered by the ECC the new European constitution was signed. However, within the next two years 25 parliaments and at least 11 referendums in the member states of the EU (at the time of writing) will determine its future (www.europa.eu.int). It seems probable that the media's representation of Europe will have at least some sort of impact on the outcome of this process. Media discourse on Europe must thus remain the focus of linguistic analyses, if applied linguistics is to take part in 'reconfiguring Europe'.

Notes

1 For instance, teenagers throughout Europe report that they gain their knowledge about Europe predominantly from the media (Convery et al., 1997: 4).

2 Thompson and Hunston's (2000) definition is similar to Biber's concept of 'social evaluation' (1988: 32). Attitude/opinion in itself is a notion that is notoriously difficult to define (and no attempt to do so will be undertaken here) (see van Dijk, 1998: 29ff for one proposal).

3 Small capitals are used for evaluative parameters.

4 There is no one-to-one equivalence between the notions in the same vertical row: the respective researchers often comprise different aspects under a similar term. One might also mention Graham's (2003) 'evaluative dimensions' and Vestergaard's (2000) types of 'Assessives', i.e. illocutions 'whose truth can [...] not be established by empirical investigation, and which ultimately rely on human assessment' (Vestergaard, 2000: 158ff).

5 A more detailed explanation of the parameter-based framework can be found in Bednarek (2006).

6 The corpus used in this research was compiled from text in newspaper articles supplied by the Lexis-Nexis service during the time I was a researcher at the University of Birmingham.

7   In analysing concordance lines I have excluded those occurrences that were not
     related to Europe as well as evaluations that were attributed to a Sayer other than
     the speaker (where this was clear from the concordance).

8   In the British context, *federal* has clear negative connotations, implying central-
     ism and threats to sovereignty (Musolff, 1996: 16–19). As Teubert points out
     '[t]he '*f*' word [...] denotes the core issue of British Euro-scepticism' (Teubert,
     2001: 51). On the debate on federalism in the British context see Mautner (2000:
     217–44).

9   *France* and *Germany* are two of the many keywords of the ECC as shown by a
     comparison with the *BNC baby* (a four million-word corpus including conversa-
     tion, academic prose, written fiction and newspaper discourse distributed by
     the Research Technologies Services of Oxford University Computing Services),
     using the wordlist function of Wordsmith Tools. Findings by Mautner suggest
     that France and Germany are the nations most frequently mentioned in British
     newspaper discourse on Europe (Mautner, 2000: 265). This derives from the
     fact that 'it is these two nations that are often considered the driving force or
     the 'heart' of the European process' (Weiss, 2002: 62). Mautner also analyses
     typical stereotypes about Germany and France that are expressed in British
     newspaper discourse (Mautner, 2000: 267–311).

References

Bakhtin, M. M. (1986) *Speech Genres and Other Late Essays*. Austin:
    University of Texas Press.
Bednarek, M. A. (2006) Evaluation in media discourse. Analysis of a newspaper
    corpus. London, New York: Continuum.
Bell, A. (1991) *The Language of News Media*. Oxford: Blackwell.
Biber, D. (1988) *Variation across Speech and Writing*. Cambridge: Cambridge
    University Press.
Biber, D. and Finegan, E. (1989) Styles of stance in English: lexical and gram-
    matical marking of evidentiality and affect. *Text* 9: 93–124.
Biber, D., Johansson, S., Leech, G., Conrad, S. and Finegan, E. (1999) *Longman
    Grammar of Spoken and Written English*. London: Longman.
Bondi, M. and Mauranen, A. (eds) (2003) *Journal of English for Academic
    Purposes* 2(4) (Special issue on evaluation in academic discourse).
Caldas-Coulthard, C. R. (2003) Cross-cultural representation of 'otherness'
    in media discourse. In G. Weiss and R. Wodak (eds) *Critical Discourse
    Analysis. Theory and Interdisciplinarity* 273–96. Houndmills: Palgrave
    Macmillan.
Clayman, S. E. (1990) From talk to text: newspaper accounts of reporter-source
    interactions. *Media, Culture and Society* 12: 79–103.
Coffin, C. and O'Halloran, K. (2004) Investigating news representations of the
    New Europe: using critical discourse analysis and a specialised corpus.
    Presentation given at BAAL 2004.

Conrad, S. and Biber, D. (2000) Adverbial marking of stance in speech
and writing. In S. Hunston and G. Thompson (eds) *Evaluation in Text.
Authorial Stance and the Construction of Discourse* 56–73. Oxford: Oxford
University Press.

Convery, A., Evans, M., Green, S., Macaro, E. and Mellor, J. (1997) An investi-
gative study into pupils' perceptions of Europe. *Journal of Multilingual and
Multicultural Development* 18(1): 1–16.

European Union. Gateway website: http://www.europa.eu.int

Florack, A. and Piontkowski, U. (2000) Acculturation attitudes of the Dutch
and the Germans towards the European Union: the importance of national
and European identification. *Journal of Multilingual and Multicultural
Development* 21(1): 1–13.

Francis, G. (1995) Corpus-driven grammar and its relevance to the learning of
English in a cross-cultural situation. Manuscript.

Good, C., Musolff, A., Points, P. and Wittlinger, R. (2001) Attitudes towards
Europe – Einstellungen zu Europa. In A. Musolff, C. Good, P. Points and
R. Wittlinger (eds) *Attitudes Towards Europe. Language in the Unification
Process* xi–xvii. Aldershot etc.: Ashgate.

Graddol, D. and Thomas, S. (eds) (1995) *Language in a Changing Europe.
Papers from the Annual Meeting of the British Association for Applied
Linguistics.* (Held at the University of Salford, September 1993) Clevedon
etc.: Multilingual Matters Ltd. (in association with BAAL).

Graham, P. (2003) Critical discourse analysis and evaluative meaning: inter-
disciplinarity as a critical turn. In G. Weiss and R. Wodak (eds) *Critical
Discourse Analysis. Theory and Interdisciplinarity* 110–29. Houndmills:
Palgrave Macmillan.

Halliday, M. A. K. (1994) *An Introduction to Functional Grammar.* London:
Edward Arnold.

Hardt-Mautner, G. (1995) 'Only connect.' Critical discourse analysis and corpus
linguistics. Manuscript, University of Lancaster. Retrieved 5 May 2004
from http://www.comp.lancs.ac.uk/computing/research/ucrel/papers/techpa-
per/vol6.pdf

Hoey, M. (2004) Lexical priming and the properties of text. Retrieved 20
November 2004 from http://www.monabaker.com/tsresources/LexicalPrimi
ngandthePropertiesofText.htm

Lemke, J. L. (1998) Resources for attitudinal meaning: evaluative orientations
in text semantics. *Functions of Language* 5: 33–56.

Lexis-Nexis, the University of Birmingham. Information from: http://www.
is.bham.ac.uk/ppm/publications/database/commerce/lexis.pdf

Macken-Horarik, M. and Martin. J. R. (eds) (2003) *Text* 23 (Special issue on
negotiating heteroglossia: social perspectives on evaluation).

Martin, J. R. (2000) Beyond exchange: appraisal systems in English. In S.
Hunston and G. Thompson (eds) *Evaluation in Text. Authorial Stance and
the Construction of Discourse* 142–75. Oxford: Oxford University Press.

Martin, J. R. and White, P. R. (2005) *The Language of Evaluation: Appraisal in English*. London/New York: Palgrave Macmillan.

Mautner, G. (2000) *Der britische Europa-Diskurs. Methodenreflexion und Fallstudien zur Berichterstattung in der Tagespresse*. Wien: Passagen Verlag.

Mautner, G. (2001) British national identity in the European context. In A. Musolff, C. Good, P. Points and R. Wittlinger (eds) *Attitudes Towards Europe. Language in the Unification Process* 3–22. Aldershot etc.: Ashgate.

Musolff, A. (1996) False friends borrowing the right words? Common terms and metaphors in European communication. In A. Musolff, C. Schäffner and M. Townson (eds) *Conceiving of Europe – Diversity in Unity* 15–30. Dartmouth: Aldershot.

Musolff, A., Schäffner, C. and Townson, M. (eds) (1996) *Conceiving of Europe – Diversity in Unity*. Dartmouth: Aldershot.

Oxford University Computing Services. Research Technologies Services website: http://www.natcorp.ox.ac.uk

Scott, M. (1999) *Wordsmith Tools*. Oxford: Oxford University Press.

Sinclair, J. (2004) A tool for text explication. In J. Sinclair (2004) *Trust the Text. Language, Corpus and Discourse* 115–27. London/New York: Routledge.

Teubert, W. (2001) A province of a federal superstate, ruled by an unelected bureaucracy – keywords of the Euro-sceptic discourse in Britain. In A. Musolff, C. Good, P. Points and R. Wittlinger (eds) *Attitudes Towards Europe. Language in the Unification Process* 45–88. Aldershot etc.: Ashgate.

Thompson, G. (1994) *Collins COBUILD English Guides 5: Reporting*. London: Harper Collins.

Thompson, G. and Hunston, S. (2000) Evaluation: an introduction. In S. Hunston and G. Thompson (eds) *Evaluation in Text: authorial stance and the construction of discourse* 1–27. Oxford: Oxford University Press.

van Dijk, T. A. (1998) Opinions and ideologies in the press. In A. Bell and P. Garret (eds) *Approaches to Media Discourse* 21.–63. Oxford/Malden, MA: Blackwell.

Vestergaard, T. (2000) From genre to sentence: the leading article and its linguistic realisation. In F. Ungerer (ed.) *English Media Texts Past and Present. Language and Textual Structure* 151–76. Amsterdam/Philadelphia: John Benjamins.

Weiss, G. (2002) Searching for Europe: the problem of legitimisation and representation in recent political speeches on Europe. *Journal of Language and Politics* 1: 59–83.

White, P. R. (2002) Appraisal. In J. Verschueren, J.-O. Östman, J. Blommaert and C. Bulcaen (eds) *Handbook of Pragmatics* 1–27. Amsterdam/Philadelphia: John Benjamins.

10   Use of language: a sign and cause of alienation

Natalie Braber

Abstract

Even 13 years after unification it seems as if the two Germanies have not yet been truly united. Since the end of the German division language has been used to illustrate the social, political and economic changes that have occurred at and since this time. This started initially in 1989 with the slogans used in the demonstrations in many cities of the German Democratic Republic (GDR) and can be seen as the first true liberated use of the national variety of German spoken in the GDR. After the initial euphoria of the Wende started to wear off, the divisions between east and west Germans started to show.[1] The asymmetry of German unification is illustrated by the influx of new vocabulary (both from west Germany and neologisms) which affected the former GDR citizens to a far greater extent than their west German neighbours. This alien-ated the two populations from one another, creating ever greater divides. The continuing division can be seen to exist (and is maintained by many east and west Germans) to this day with the maintenance of GDR vocabulary, ideas and stereotypes furthering the psychological wall which still separates the Germans. West Germans have not been affected by these changes to the same extent. By examining these different attitudes and relationships a clearer light can be shed upon the difficulties confronting the Germans and this may enable a smoother future for Germany.

1   Introduction

German unification in 1990 brought together two German-speaking populations which for the previous 45 years had been establishing different and often oppos-ing political systems, economies, social institutions and cultures. Although separation was never complete, communication between the two populations had been severely hampered. As a result of separate political, economic, social and cultural developments, and the lack of communication, changes occurred in the German language which were specific to each of these populations. These changes came to light in language and intercultural communication problems after 1989, notably when the citizens of the former East and West Germanies came face-to-face after years of segregation.

The development of the German language since 1945 has been the subject of extensive research. This research has concentrated on general developments as well as specific aspects of language. Linguists, such as Manfred Hellmann (1984, 1989, 1995), Wolf Oschlies (1981, 1989), Norbert Dittmar (1997) and Ruth Reiher (1993, 1996, 2000), Ulla Fix (1994, 1997), Herberg et al. (1997) and Patrick Stevenson (1997, 2002), to name but a few, have comprehensively examined a wide range of topics, often covering social as well as linguistic changes. Some linguists, such as Leo Hoppert (1990) and Ewald Lang (1990) have reviewed specific aspects of language in greater detail, for instance political slogans used by the demonstrators in 1989 in the GDR, while Dieter Herberg and his colleagues (1997) have studied media language from East and West Germany, as well as unified Germany, to investigate changes in the economic and political spheres of language. The language interest shifted from looking at the different 'varieties' of German as linguists were examining the effects that unification would have on the language.

2   Situation in Germany around 1990

Many changes which had taken place came to light when the citizens of East and West Germany were re-united after years of separation. Linguistically, the situation pre-1989 showed that most changes within the different varieties of German involved lexical items. Although general comprehension was still intact, there were differences between East and West German varieties (Antos & Schubert, 1997: 308). The post-1989 situation has been quite different, as Michael Clyne comments: 'if there had not been a GDR national variety, the convergence discussed in this chapter would not be necessary … the process of divergence has stopped. The reversal is in progress, involving innovation, disintegration of past structures, and integration to the West' (Clyne, 1995: 87). Initially, feelings of euphoria were felt by many; the events of November 1989 were so sudden and unexpected, for both those in East and West, that nobody could believe what was happening. At this time, very few people publicly considered the differences between East and West, and what the future would bring.[2] But, for many, the joy was short-lived. Although the political division of the two Germanies ended after the fall of the Wall, the social and cultural situation of the majority of the population of Germany did not change immediately. Furthermore, all the years of separation had resulted in a mentality both in East and West in which each regarded the other as foreigners. Creutziger comments that the communication problems between the people of the former East and West Germanies were not solely due to their past, but that there were new forms of 'separatism' forming, held by many from the East and from the West (Creutziger, 1997: 89). It was felt, for example, in the former GDR that the people of the Federal Republic of Germany (FRG) had not shown much interest in the life of East Germans during the time of the division. Another major perceived and real problem of unification was that it was not a symmetrical union, both on the political and individual level. On the political level, the GDR was incorporated into the FRG on the basis of the West German constitution. On the individual level, both states had different preconceptions and desires of unification and these were very hard to reconcile. This became obvious when the people of the two German states were forced to confront each other, for example, Baudusch writes that the linguistic differences were not cancelled out by unification, but became even more noticeable (Baudusch, 1995: 313). Simple everyday aspects of life in a capitalist economy had to be learned by the people of the east: how to write a business letter, curriculum vitae or letter of reference. Similarly, issues related to finding accommodation and employment, which were familiar for westerners, could become major problems for easterners.

Each side tended to blame the other for negative developments outside their control. Looking at the perceived advantages the others had gained, each side emphatically believed that the other side had got more out of unification than themselves. According to a questionnaire carried out by Wagner in 1999, 75% of all west Germans said that unification had more disadvantages than advantages for them, while 75% of all east Germans thought that the west Germans had received more. Wagner comments that this is not a good basis for understanding (Wagner, 1999: 24). Many opinions were based on stereotypes and clichés. For example, in Bittermann's outspoken book, *It's a Zoni*, Tietz writes an article about the friction between the people of east and west Germany. He writes that people were strangers to each other both before and after unification, and felt that they knew nothing about those who had lived on the other side of the Wall. He mentions that there were feelings of confusion about the east Germans: about their different clothes and hairstyles, as well as their behaviour and that these feelings towards them sometimes extended to hate. According to Tietz, rather than belonging and growing together, ten years after unification, east and west Germany were further apart from each other than ever before (Tietz, 1999: 39).

3   New vocabulary for East Germany (post-1989)

The citizens of the GDR were put under pressure to conform to west German values, frequently by west German politicians and business leaders, but in many cases also by their own people. It was thought by many east Germans that the only way to advance was to adopt West German practices, and that all East German practices had to be discarded. Some east Germans managed quickly to adapt to the new ways and they felt comfortable with their new life, but for others it created a deep loss of identity, inferiority complexes and even identity crises (e.g. Kramer, 1996; Förster & Roski, 1990). Many east Germans began to feel resentful of the manner in which they and their heritage were treated, and, in addition to feeling like second-class citizens, they began to develop a sense of nostalgia, a phenomenon which became popularly known as *Ostalgie*, a word-play on the German word for nostalgia, which is '*Nostalgie*' (for example Becker et al., 1992, and actual description of the word *Ostalgie* in Kramer, 1998: 279). There was widespread regret that the positive features of the GDR had not been preserved, such as the social support or housing situations. For many east Germans, unification had not been a primary goal of the demonstrations which took place in the GDR in the autumn of 1989. Many wanted a democratic state, which would still be separate from the FRG (Fulbrook, 1992: 83). These people wanted to keep the spirit of the GDR alive within the new Germany. At a time of sudden and rapid changes a single group identity becomes an important aspect of life, as many people feel the need to 'belong' to a community. Heneghan explains the need among east Germans for a common identity: 'This [e]ast German identity is now a symbolic construction, a reaction to the way that everything became different at once. People need an anchor to hold them steady during this radical upheaval' (Heneghan, 2000: 149).

The political, economic, social and cultural issues described above have influenced the development of the German language in different ways. Prior to 1989, linguists debated the question to what extent the German language was changing and whether this would lead to the formation of two different languages or national varieties. The conclusion of this debate was that the varieties used in the two German states would not become foreign to each other, although growing differences in vocabulary were inevitable[3] especially in the areas of politics and economics. It was, for example, found by the late 1980s that about two thousand new words had been formed which were used solely in the GDR (Baudusch, 1995: 304). In some cases different words were used for the same concepts as in the FRG, such as *Herrentag* instead of *Himmelfahrt* (Ascension Day), in other cases, words were needed to describe

GDR-specific terms, such as *Erster Sekretär* for the President of the GDR. Many GDR-specific words were acronyms, such as *FDJ* (*Freie Deutsche Jugend* which was a youth group) or *VOPO* (*Volkspolizist* for policeman) which made such terms difficult to understand for any outsiders. At the same time, many new words which were forming in the FRG related to technological and commercial innovation, frequently influenced by American and British English. Differences in language usage also added to such problems, for example, the phrase *Heute im Angebot* (special offer today) in the FRG meant that a product was available at reduced price whereas in the GDR it meant that a product was available. The foundation for communication difficulties in the unified Germany was laid.

Furthermore, events such as the fall of the Wall and the unification of Germany led to the creation of new words. Novel words, or novel meanings, were needed to describe the new situation in Germany, for example *die Wende*, which was the word which signalled the change from communism to capitalism was used with a new meaning at this time.[4] In other cases, where an existing word had different meanings in each state or when two different words had the same meaning, a choice had to be made. However, it tended to be the East German meaning of the word or the East German word which was lost. There was little or no movement of words from east to west. Words like *Mauerspecht* (used to describe people who chipped off chunks of the Wall to sell), *Zwei-Plus-Vier-Gespräch* (to refer to political discussions which were taking place) and *Stasi-Auflösung* (the dissolving of the GDR secret police) were new to both sides. These were mainly words which were needed to describe the new political and social situations in Germany. Many of these words are presently already out of use in Germany as they were only needed to describe the situation at that time. But even for these new words there seemed to be a difference for east and west Germans. Most of the neologisms affected what was happening in the former GDR, as it was here where most of the changes were taking place. These new concepts did not seem to affect the lives of FRG citizens to as great an extent. Words like *Treuhand* (to do with the privatising the state-owned business of the GDR), *Seilschaft* (referring to former GDR politicians who used their former positions to gain new positions in unified Germany) and *Abwicklung* (the liquidation of businesses) were known to west Germans but they did not affect their lives directly. However, many of these neologisms had life-changing meanings for east Germans, and were often perceived in a negative way. Many of these new words, as well as the related processes came to be hated in East Germany: *Abwicklung*, became one of the most hated words of German bureaucracy. The free market economy which was imposed on east Germany was reflected in many such terms. In the world of business and commerce, many West German words were adopted in the east. Many political terms of the GDR were no longer used as the political system which required them collapsed, and the new *Länder* (German states) used West German political vocabulary.

4   Loss of GDR-specific vocabulary

At the time of the fall of the Wall most linguists expected that the national variety used in the GDR would be lost after 1990 (e.g. Ahrends, 1990; Bergmann, 1995). This is explained by Bergmann, who questions whether words are no longer used because they are out of date or because the actual object being described has become obsolete (Bergmann, 1995: 18). Immediately after unification, many east Germans were indeed keen to avoid the language of the former GDR to reduce the possibility of being pigeon-holed. The first changes in language took place in the sphere of politics, and as the official language of the leading party in the GDR (the *Sozialistische Einheitspartei Deutschlands*) had been so rigid, these differences were especially noticeable, with alterations being made in official discourse, for example on radio and television and in newspapers. But, as the initial euphoria of belonging to a united Germany wore off, many words which had been used in East Germany were brought into use again. This is an example of language being used symbolically to emphasise the nature and identity of the speaker as many east Germans became more hesitant in taking over all aspects of west German language, for example using words like *Plastetüte* instead of *Plastikbeutel* for a plastic carrier bag (see also Schönfeld, 1993: 201). In addition, some East German words had to be used to describe former institutions that did not exist in the West, while other East German vocabulary was so ingrained in peoples' minds, and part of their everyday lives, that it was difficult for them to eradicate it completely. People also needed to use this language to describe the effect changes were having on their present lives. A few East German traditions continued to be carried out in unified Germany. The *Jugendweihe*, for example, which is similar to a non-religious confirmation is still taken by many east Germans. According to Kauke, 50% of all young people in east Germany were still taking part in this ceremony in 1997 (Kauke, 1997: 374) and this still continues in Germany today.

Although only about 2,000 words used solely in East Germany were shown to have existed before 1989 and many of these started to disappear gradually after the Wall fell (Baudusch, 1995: 304), their usage did lead to some confusion. Communication breakdowns, for example, occurred because people used certain words in different ways and attached different meanings to them, for example words like *Eigentum* (property) and *Sozialismus* (socialism) which had very different connotations for speakers in the two states (see for example Hellmann, 1991 and 1997, Lerchner, 1996 and Reiher and Baumann, 2000).

5   Alienation and nostalgia

At the time when many east Germans were feeling disillusioned with the situation in Germany, the link between language and identity became very apparent and former varieties of words which had been used by speakers in the GDR were 'resurrected'. Words which were not ideologically loaded were reintroduced and regularly used, for example with East Germans using the terms *Kaufhalle* instead of *Supermarkt* and *Broiler* instead of *Brathähnchen* (for a roast chicken). In some restaurants in East Berlin there are signs saying '*Hier können Sie Broiler sagen*'. GDR nostalgia also witnessed a resurgence of 'patriotism' in the marketing world, where place of origin in the GDR was stressed in advertising features. Immediately after the Wall fell, many East German products had disappeared from the market, but many of these returned to the market, particularly after 1993 when confidence in the 'new' Germany was at a low ebb, and this was underlined in advertising campaigns. Advertising agencies used terms which were familiar to their customers and many slogans contained phrases such as *unser* (our) as well as stating place of produce as being the former GDR (Richmond, Kolbe & Kolbe, 1995: 362). Stevenson comments that by late 1991 around 75% of east Germans claimed to prefer east German products (Stevenson, 2002: 226).

To express feelings about each other and to emphasise group identity, people of East and West had created names for each other and for them-selves. The most basic of these words are *Ossi* and *Wessi*, with others being more offensive, for example, some West Germans refer to East Germans as *Einheimische Ost* ('natives' in a pejorative sense), *Ostpocke* (Eastern 'pox' as in smallpox), and *Udo*, which stood for *Unsere doofe Ossis* (our stupid Ossis). The East Germans had fewer names for those from the West, but some of those in use were *die Eingebildeten* (the conceited ones), *die da drüben* (those on the other side) and occasionally *Westschweine* (Westpigs) (Herberg et al., 1997 discuss many of these terms in detail). These names did not help the relationship between the people of east and west. Frequently east Germans felt a need to differentiate themselves from the west Germans and often referred to their lives as *bei uns in der DDR* or *bei uns im Osten* (both of these terms emphasising 'our' GDR). This continued usage after unification reinforced the mental barrier and illustrated the fact that the people of east Germany did not feel fully integrated into unified Germany. Already before 1989 there were many different terms to refer to East and West Germany from both sides, but these terms emphasised the reluctance of both states to fully recognise the other (see Richmond et al., 1995 and Stevenson, 2002: 50 in particular for more details). Wagner describes their reaction as a return to the features which had dominated their lives in the GDR but were felt to be less important at the time of the *Wende*: equality and solidarity (Wagner, 1999: 159). Dittmar comments on the fact that each side developed names to call the other because the majority of people found they could not cross the barriers of difference which separated them. He writes that people of the former East and West felt they were strangers to each other and that the years of separation could not be overcome (Dittmar & Bredel, 1999: 64).

In short, as time went on after the fall of the Wall, language used was more crucial in east Germany than in west Germany. Using East German words became a way of making a statement. Dittmar and Bredel comment on this usage of East German vocabulary, stating that those who used East German words were coming out as *Ossis*, those who do not use it were losing part of their language. They comment that there was no such thing as remaining neutral (Dittmar & Bredel, 1999: 138).

Often it is in the spoken language that statements of identity can be made. In addition to using special words, speakers have other ways of expressing an identity, for example, by speaking in dialect. The usage of the dialect of Berlin, *Berlinisch*, illustrates this. Throughout the GDR, *Berlinisch* was seen as a dialect of the workers, which had a very positive role in the socialist state and was considered a prestige variety (Schmidt-Regener, 1999 and Stevenson, 2002). For many East Germans this dialect signalled a difference between the people and the GDR politicians, many of whom were from Saxony and therefore had a different dialect. Berliners used this dialect in all areas of life, including in the workplace, schools and universities. In West Berlin though, this dialect was frowned upon and tended to be avoided in public. Especially after unification, *Berlinisch* became a way of identifying oneself with the people of the former GDR and was used throughout the east, not just in east Berlin (Schmidt-Regener, 1999).

6   Modal particles

Another, perhaps more unconscious, way of making a statement in spoken language is the use of modal particles. Adler was unusual for his time as he defines modal particles as an integral part of language, not merely a trend, words which round off a sentence and make it flow more cleanly (Adler, 1964: 54). Linguistic research long disregarded modal particles as they were not considered to have a specific function in language (Baerentzen,

1989: 19). This is shown by the names modal particles were previously given in the German language, including *Fügewörter, Sprachhülsen, unscheinbare Kleinwörter, sinnlose Einschiebsel, Parasiten* and *Läuse im Pelz der Sprache* (which can be translated as addition words, language shells, insignificant little words, meaningless insertions, parasites and lice in the fur of language). Not only were they considered unimportant, but linguists could also not decide to which word class these words belonged. Often many groups of uninflected words were grouped together under one heading. However, eventually it was established that modal particles have an important function, particularly in the spoken language, where they can be considered a crucial feature (Burkhardt, 1982: 153). Modal particles are now credited with playing an important role in spoken language, even though their exact role has been difficult to describe.

Modal particles tend to be used to illustrate the speaker's opinion of what he or she is saying. They express the subjective opinion of the speaker and can highlight involvement of the speaker. They do not alter the truth value of a sentence and they can be removed from a sentence without affecting its grammaticality (Helbig & Helbig, 1995: 9). Most modal particles have more than one function, and it is extremely difficult to give each modal particle an individual meaning, as they can change in context (Brausse, 1986: 206; König, 1977: 116–7; Krivonosov, 1965: 574). However, they are not meaningless fillers but are a crucial part of the meaning of spoken language (for example the differences between *Wie heißt du, wie heißt du denn, wie heißt du eigentlich* for 'what's your name' where such modal particles can be used in conjunction with pitch and emphasis to either harden or soften such questions).

The 1995 corpus of interviews carried out in the early 1990s with citizens of east and west Berlin (there are 29 interviews with people from east Berlin and 24 from west Berlin) collected by students of Norbert Dittmar of the Free University (Berlin) offers an opportunity to compare the use of modal particles in the east and the west. The interviews, held six years after the fall of the Wall, asked interviewees about the night of the 9 November 1989 when the Berlin Wall fell, and they were also asked how their lives had changed since this time and what they thought about the situation in Germany since unification.[5]

The Dittmar corpus was interesting as it stirred especially deep emotions in the east Berlin speakers and would allow comparison between this group and the west Berlin group acting as a control as many of these speakers were less emotional about this topic. Other research carried out by the author (Braber, 2001, 2006) revealed a strong relation between emotion and the use of modal particles. The occurrence of modal particles was calculated in the following way. As the east Berlin interviews were slightly longer, the modal particles were counted as an average per page of the transcript and not as an absolute number. This allowed for an examination of the average use of modal particles across the groups as well as the individual and allowed the examination of any speakers who were using modal particles in a way that was statistically significant from their group average. The description of the fall of the Wall and the perceived discrimination against the citizens of the former GDR often stirred the emotions of the interviewees. During these moments which were classed as particularly emotional (by looking at features such as subject content, as well as non-linguistic features such as heavier breathing patterns, noisy swallowing and quickened tempo – which were all noticed by the interviewers during the interviews and verified by the author) the frequency of modal particles' use rose considerably. This phenomenon appeared in all population groups (there was a representative sample of gender and age. Occupation, however, was not evenly distributed with many interviewees being teachers. These are, however, a particularly interesting sample as teachers would be more used to speaking to an audience and one would expect them to be more aware of their language use). This was both true for east and west Berlin speakers, but as the situation of unification had affected most west Berlin speakers to a lesser extent, this emotional heightening was not as common throughout the speakers.

The interviews also show that in general people of east and west Berlin use different modal particles, but that the use of these modal particles is changing. The modal particles *eben* and *halt* (they have many functions but some of these are that they can emphasise an inescapable conclusion; have the sense of exactly, precisely or just; and they can add a sense of unalterability), for example, were used differently during the years of division and their usage has changed significantly since unification, predominantly among the speakers from the former GDR (Dittmar, 1999; Braber, 2001). It can be seen in the interviews that the German speakers in west Berlin used *halt* to a similar extent as *eben*, but this is not the case for the east Berlin speakers. The modal particle *halt* was traditionally considered to be the South German variant of *eben*. This is illustrated by Hentschel by showing usage of both *eben* and *halt* in Germany in the 1980s (Hentschel, 1986: 175). *Halt* was for many years considered a prestige variety in North Germany and many West Germans outside North Germany adopted the usage of this modal particle. This usage spread to West Berlin in the years before the Wall fell. It is clear from the data that since reunification the usage of *halt* has slowly started to spread to the younger citizens of east Berlin and east Germany. This is the case as some of the youngest speakers (late teenage years and early twenties) are using the *halt* form but very few of the speakers any older than this are using it. In the 1970s and 1980s the modal particle *halt* was not found in Brandenburg, Berlin or other areas of the GDR. During the years of the GDR many people in the East would have avoided using the modal particle *halt* as it suggested deviation from the East German norm towards a West German markedness, which most speakers would have wanted to avoid.

At the time of the interviews it can be seen that the modal particle *halt* was still exceptional in east Berlin, and even today its usage within these interviews could suggest a sense of identification with west Berlin and west Germany. Some of the younger speakers in the corpus mention that using *halt* can be seen as a desire to integrate into western society. The majority of the east German citizens who were interviewed for the Dittmar corpus did not use *halt*. However, the fact, that by 1995 the youngest interviewees who came from the former GDR had started to use *halt* shows a change from the period before 1990 which is illustrated in Hentschel's map showing previous usage (Hentschel, 1986: 175). Stevenson (2002: 156) has commented on several weaknesses of the conclusions that Dittmar and Bredel (1999) draw from these data as they used overall numbers from the interviews. This research has tried to combat these problems by working out average uses of the modal particles rather than an overall figure as the interviews were of such differing lengths.[6]

Measuring the number of modal particles used in the Dittmar corpus suggests a greater usage of modal particles by people from the former GDR. More than one reason can be suggested for such a feature. It may be a sign of greater dialect usage in the east. Modal particles and tags are often part of dialect and a different way of speaking. Perhaps the interviewees from the former GDR used more modal particles and tags because they lived in a society where, among friends, a more co-operative style of dialogue was used, rather than the more aggressive style of speaking which many east Germans feel west Germans have. However, the use of modal particles among east German speakers may also reflect the fact that they feel less secure in their new position in a unified Germany.[7] Maybe the relatively greater usage of modal particles suggests that interviewees seek feedback from the interviewer. There are many uses for modal particles and it does seem that they apply to the interviews which were analysed. However, the interesting fact remains that the frequency of modal particle usage increased at emotional parts of the interview. The west Berlin group were acting as a control group as their reports were not as emotional and this allowed the investigation to examine the correlation between the features of emotionality and modal particles.

Modal particles also highlight another development. We have already seen that, although *eben* is more common in east Berlin and east Germany, the situation is changing slowly as east Germans, especially the younger people interviewed were more closely involved with west Germans in the workplace are starting to adopt the traditional South German variant *halt*. This adoption is similar to the adoption which spread throughout west Germany over the last decades and where the two varieties now co-exist. In this, there is an obvious similarity with general language trends in Germany. West Berliners and west Germans rarely pick up the east German words, and this reflects the general movement of language from west to east which was illustrated earlier in this article. The data on the usage of *eben* and *halt* suggest that, even though contact between the two sides is growing in a gradual process of social and linguistic unification, language movement remains uni-directional.

7   Conclusion

In conclusion, it can be said that the years of separation, the lack of communication and the new problems which arose after unification affect the lives of people in both east and west Germany. An on-going process of political, economic, social and cultural change is reflected in their usage of spoken German. At the same time, language is used both consciously and subconsciously to emphasize perceived and real problems and group identification. The building of a new relationship between the population from east and west is hampered by language and intercultural communication problems. The question is whether the people of the 'new' Germany are in some cases looking for differences rather than similarities to use this in illustrating the greater differences between east and west. Kramer writes that, since the fall of the Wall in 1989, many different people have referred to a new wall, one which cannot be overcome. This new wall is a psychological one, it exists within peoples' heads and is separating the Germans (Kramer, 1996: 55). To break this wall down, linguists can make a contribution. By making people more aware of what separates and unites them, they can encourage tolerance and acceptance. More research remains to be done, but creating a better understanding of language and intercultural communication[8] can help solve problems in contemporary Germany, whether these are purely linguistic or more deeply ingrained within German attitudes towards one another.

Notes

1   In order to avoid confusion, I will refer to the two German states as East and West German when referring to the pre-1989 situation and as east and west German for present day references. This follows the convention set by Stevenson and Theobald (2000).

2   Such opinions were expressed by many of the participants of the Dittmar corpus which will be examined at a later point in this article.

3   For information regarding the German situation before 1989, see Andersson (1984), Dieckmann (1989) and Lerchner (1974), although there is a vast literature regarding this time. For the situation after 1989 there is also a very comprehensive literature but to name just a few: Baudusch (1995), Hellmann (1990) and Creutziger (1997).

4   There were many words used to describe the situation at this time (*Revolution, Umbruch, Wandel* etc.) but the word *Wende* came to be symbolic for this time and did not have to compete with any of the other words. It came to be used with the definite article *die Wende* which further illustrates this fact. The word *Wende* had been used before, in June 1953, when the SED tried to signal a new, more liberal trend, and it had also been used by Kohl in West Germany after the end of the socialist-liberal coalition, when he talked of the changes which would take place. The first published use of *Wende* in its new form was on 5 October 1989 in a *Vereinigte Linke* text (an East German party). It was used in inverted commas because of this new association. After Egon Krenz, Erich Honecker's successor as leader of the SED, used it on 18 October 1989 it became a catchword of the *SED* for a couple of weeks. For a further description of *Wende* and linked words, see Herberg et al., 1997 and for the quote from the initial text, see page 81. See also Stevenson, 2002: 93.

5   There are other corpora collected around this time but these were not as suitable for this research. Kühn and Almstädt (1997) compared work references and Reiher (1997) examined adverts for housing vacancies. These are both concerned with written texts which would have left little scope for examining modal particles. Antos and Schubert (1997) examined advice sessions held by phone. This corpus was considered unsuitable for this research as there was an inequality between the two sides, with west Germans being the advice-givers and east Germans the advice-takers which would not have allowed for a direct comparison. Finally, Auer, Birkner and Kern's (1997) analysis of real and role-play interviews was considered unsuitable as it involved a formal language style, giving less scope for looking at modal particles.

6   Dittmar and Bredel also comment on the extent to which *eben* can be seen as the 'harder' equivalent to *halt*. However, this is not an area that is to be commented on here, as overall usage is the main focus.

7   Antos and Richter examine the concept of east German *Sprachlosigkeit* which ties in with this (Antos & Richter, 2000).

8   Stevenson comments that the notion of 'intercultural' and 'interculturality' are not clear. He comments 'if communicative obstacles are found to be no greater and no more systematic between east and west Germans than, say, between Hamburgers and Bavarians, the ground for claiming 'interculturality' are not clear ... being east or west German is therefore not a sufficient condition for interaction between two parties to be construed as intercultural, nor is it merely

a matter of identifying different communicative practices: the differences have
to derive from, and be actively associated with, incompatible features of the
participants' respective life experiences' (Stevenson, 2002: 235).

References

Adler, H. G. (1964) Füllwörter. *Muttersprache* 74: 52–5.
Ahrends, M. (1990) Kleine DDR-Sprachschule (1). *Die Zeit* 9–23 February.
Andersson, S-G.(1984) Wortwanderung. Zur Beschreibung der deutsch-deut-
    schen Sprachsituation im Bereich des Wortschatzes. *Deutsche Sprache* 12:
    54–84.
Antos, G. and Richter, S. (2000) ‚Sprachlosigkeit' Ost? Anmerkungen aus lin-
    guistischer Sicht. In G. Jackman and I. Roe (eds) *Finding a Voice. Problems
    of Language in East German Society and Culture* 75–96. Amsterdam:
    Rodopi.
Antos, G. and Schubert, T. (1997) Unterschiede in kommunikativen Mustern
    zwischen Ost und West. *Zeitschrift für Germanistische Linguistik* 25:
    308–30.
Auer, P., Birkner, K. and Kern, F. (1997) Wörter – Formeln – Argumente. Was in
    Bewerbungsgesprächen ‚Spaß' macht. In I. Barz and U. Fix (eds) *Deutsch-
    deutsche Kommunikationserfahrungen im arbeitsweltlichen Alltag* 213–231.
    Heidelberg: Universitätsverlag C Winter.
Baerentzen, P. (1989) Syntaktische Subklassifizierung der Fügewörter im
    Deutschen. In H. Weydt (ed.) *Sprechen mit Partikeln* 19–29. Berlin: Walter
    de Gruyter.
Baudusch, R. (1995) Fremdheit und Vertrautheit. *Muttersprache* 105: 302–14.
Becker, U., Becker, H. and Ruhland, W. (1992) *Zwischen Angst und
    Aufbruch. Das Lebensgefühl der Deutschen in Ost und West nach der
    Wiedervereinigung*. Düsseldorf: Econ Verlag.
Bergmann, C. (1995) Überlegungen zur historischen Schichtung des
    Wortschatzes der deutschen Sprache. In G. Lerchner, M. Schröder and U.
    Fix (eds) *Chronologische, areale und situative Varietäten des deutschen in
    der Sprachhistoriographie* 17–21. Frankfurt am Main: Peter Lang.
Braber, N. (2001) *The German Language and Reunification 1990: the effect of
    emotion on the use of modal particles in East and West Berlin*. Unpublished
    PhD thesis, St Andrews University.
Braber, N. (2006) Emotional and emotive language. Modal particles and tags in
    unified Berlin. *Journal of Pragmatics* 38: 1487–503.
Brausse, U. (1986) Zum Problem der sogenannten Polyfunktionalität von
    Modalpartikeln. Ja und eben als Argumentationssignale. *Zeitschrift für
    Phonetik, Sprachwissenschaft und Kommunikationsforschung* 39: 206–23.
Burkhardt, A. (1982) Gesprächswörter. In W. Mentrup (ed.) *Konzepte zur
    Lexikographie* 138–71. Tübingen: Max Niemeyer Verlag.
Clyne, M. (1995) *The German Language in a Changing Europe*. Cambridge:
    Cambridge University Press.

Creutziger, W. (1997) Heutiges Deutsch und neuer Separatismus. In G.
    Schmirber (ed.) *Sprache im Gespräch – zu Normen, Gebrauch und Wandel
    der deutschen Sprache* 88–93. Munich: Hanns-Seidel-Stiftung e.V.
Dieckmann, W. (1989) Die Untersuchung der deutsch-deutschen
    Sprachentwicklung als llinguistisches Problem. *Zeitschrift für
    Germanistische Linguistik* 17: 162–81.
Dittmar, N. (1997) Sprachliche und kommunikative Perspektiven auf ein
    gesamtdeutsche Ereignis in Erzählungen von Ost- und Westberlinern. In I.
    Barz and U. Fix (eds) *Deutsch-deutsche Kommunikationserfahrungen im
    arbeitsweltlichen Alltag* 1–32. Heidelberg: Universitätsverlag C. Winter.
Dittmar, N. (1999) Sozialer Umbruch und Sprachwandel am Beispiel der
    Modalpartikeln halt und eben in der Berliner Kommunikationsgemeinschaft
    nach der ‚Wende'. In P. Auer and H. Hausendorf (eds) *Kommunikation
    im gesellschaftlichen Umbruchsituationen. Mikroanalytische Aspekte des
    sprachlichen und gesellschaftlichen Wandels in den neuen Bundesländern*
    199–234. Tübingen: Max Niemeyer Verlag.
Dittmar, N. and Bredel, U. (1999) *Die Sprachmauer*. Berlin: Weidler
    Buchverlag.
Fix, U. (1994) Sprache vor und nach der ‚Wende': ‚Gewendete' Texte
    – ‚Gewendete' Textsorten. In H. J. Heringer, G. Samson, M. Kauffmann
    and W. Bader (eds) *Tendenzen der deutschen Gegenwartssprache* 131–46.
    Tübingen: Max Niemeyer Verlag.
Fix, U. (1996) Die Sicht der Betroffenen – Beobachtungen zum
    Kommunikationswandel in den neuen Bundesländern. *Der
    Deutschunterricht* 1: 34–41.
Förster, P. and Roski, G. (1990) *DDR zwischen Wende und Wahl*. Berlin:
    LinksDruck Verlag.
Fuchs, P. (1996) Freiheit wächst mit den Alternativen. Wider die Moral in der
    Differenz. In Heinrich-Böll Stiftung (eds) *Die Sprache als Hort der Freiheit*
    20–4. Cologne: Heinrich-Böll Stiftung.
Fulbrook, M. (1992) *The two Germanies 1945–1990 – Problems of
    Interpretation*. London: Macmillan.
Helbig, G. and Helbig, A. (1995) *Deutsche Partikeln – richtig gebraucht?*
    Leipzig: Langscheidt-Verlag Enzyklopädie.
Hellmann, M. W. (1984) *Ost-West-Wortschatzvergleiche*. Tübingen: Gunter Narr
    Verlag.
Hellmann, M. W. (1989) Zwei Gesellschaften – Zwei Sprachkulturen? *Forum
    für interdisziplinäre Forschung* 2: 27–38.
Hellmann, M. W. (1990) DDR-Sprachgebrauch nach der Wende – Eine erste
    Bestandaufnahme. *Muttersprache* 100: 266–86.
Hellmann, M. W. (1991) Zur vergleichenden Untersuchung alltagssprachlichen
    Handelns in den beiden deutschen Staaten. ‚Ich suche eine Wohnung'.
    Beiträge zur Sprachwissenschaft 5: 19–32.
Hellmann, M. W. (1995) Wörter der Wendezeit. *Sprachreport* 3: 14–16.

Hellmann, M. W. (1997) Sprach- und Kommunikationsprobleme in Deutschland Ost und West. In Gisela Schmirber (ed.) *Sprache im Gespräch – Zu Normen, Gebrauch und Wandel der deutschen Sprache* 53–87. Munich: Hanns-Seidel-Stiftung.

Heneghan, T. (2000) *Unchained Eagle: Germany after the wall*. London: Reuters.

Hentschel, E. (1986) *Funktion und Geschichte deutscher Partikeln*. Tübingen: Max Niemeyer Verlag.

Herberg, D., Steffens, D. and Tellenbach, E. (1997) *Schlüsselwörter der Wendezeit*. Berlin: Walter de Gruyter.

Hoppert, L. (1990) *Egon reiß die Mauer ein ... Leipziger DEMO-Sprüche*. Münster: Coppenrath Verlag.

Kauke, W. (1997) Politische Rituale als Spiegelbild des Gesellschaftlichen. Die Kommunikationskonstellation des Rituals ‚Jugendweihe‘ in der DDR und seine Entwicklung nach der Wende. In I. Barz and U. Fix (eds) *Deutsch-deutsche Kommunikationserfahrungen im arbeitsweltlichen Alltag* 367–78. Heidelberg: Universitätsverlag C. Winter.

König, E. (1977) Modalpartikeln in Fragesätzen. In H. Weydt (ed.) *Aspekte der Modalpartikeln – Studien zur deutschen Abtönung* 115–30. Tübingen: Max Niemeyer Verlag.

Kramer, U. (1996) Von Ossi-Nachweisen und Buschzulagen. (Nachwendewörter – sprachliche Ausrutscher oder bewußte Etikettierung). In R. Reiher and Undine Kramer (eds) *Von Buschzulage und Ossi-Nachweis* 55–69. Berlin: Aufbau Taschenbuch Verlag.

Kramer, U. (1998) ‚Wir und die anderen’ – Distanzierung durch Sprache. In R. Reiher and U. Kramer (eds) *Sprache als Mittel von Identifikation und Distanzierung* 273–98. Frankfurt am Main: Peter Lang.

Krivonosov, A. (1965) Die Wechselbeziehung zwischen den modalen Partikeln und der Satzintonation im Deutschen. *Zeitschrift für Phonetik, Sprachwissenschaft und Kommunikationsforschung* 18: 573–89.

Kühn, I. and Almstädt, K. (1997) Deutsch-deutsche Verständigungsprobleme. *Der Deutschunterricht* 49: 86–94.

Lang, E. (1990) *Wendehals und Stasi-Laus – Demo-Sprüche aus der DDR*. Munich: Wilhelm Heyne Verlag.

Lerchner, G. (1974) Zur Spezifik der Gebrauchsweise der deutschen Sprache in der DDR und ihrer gesellschaftlichen Determination. *Deutsch als Fremdsprache* 11: 259–65.

Lercher, G. (1996) *Sprachgebrauch im Wandel*. Frankfurt am Main: Peter Lang.

Oschlies, W. (1981) ‚Ich glaub’, mich rammt ein Rotkehlchen…’ Jugendjargon und Soziolinguistik der DDR. *Muttersprache* 98: 205–13.

Oschlies, W. (1989) *Würgende und wirkende Wörter – Deutschsprechen in der DDR*. Berlin: Verlag Gebr. Holzapfel.

Reiher, R. (1997) Dreiraum- versus Dreizimmerwohnung. *Der Deutschunterricht* 49: 42–9.

Reiher, R. and Läzer, R. (1993) *Wer spricht das wahre Deutsch?* Berlin: Aufbau Taschenbuch Verlag.

Reiher, R. and Läzer, R. (1996) *Von Buschzulage und Ossi-Nachweis.* Berlin: Aufbau Taschenbuch Verlag.

Reiher, R. and Baumann, A. (2000) *Mit gespaltener Zunge? Die deutsche Sprache nach dem Fall der Mauer.* Berlin: Aufbau Taschenbuch Verlag.

Richmond, E., Kolbe, U. and Kolbe, K. (1995) East-west semantic diversity in present-day Germany: lexica, neologisms, and collocations since reunification. *Word* 46(3): 353–67.

Schönfeld, H. (1993) Auch sprachlich beigetreten? In R. Reiher and Rüdiger Läzer (eds) *Wer spricht das wahre Deutsch?* 187–209. Berlin: Aufbau Taschenbuch Verlag.

Schmidt-Regener, I. (1999) Language attitudes in the Berlin speech community after the fall of the wall in 1989. Unpublished article which can be found on: http://www.ub.uni-konstanz.de/kops/volltexte/1999/3/47/

Stevenson, P. (1997) *The German-Speaking World. A Practical Introduction to Sociolinguistic Issues.* London: Routledge.

Stevenson, P. (2002) *Language and German Disunity. A Sociolinguistic History of East and West in Germany, 1945–2000.* Oxford: Oxford University Press.

Stevenson, P. and Theobald, J. (2000) *Discursive Disunity in Unified Germany.* London: Macmillan Press.

Tietz, F. (1999) Deutscher als alle anderen. In K. Bittermann (ed.) *It's a Zoni (Zehn Jahre Wiedervereinigung. Die Ossis als Belastung und Belästigung)* 35–9. Berlin: Edition Tiamat.

Wagner, W. (1999) *Kulturshock Deutschland – der zweite Blick.* Hamburg: Rotbuch Verlag.

Contributors

Monika Bednarek is Lecturer in English Linguistics, Dept of English Linguistics, University of Augsburg, Germany.

Natalie Braber is Lecturer in Linguistics, School of Arts, Communication and Culture, Nottingham Trent University, UK.

Guus Extra is Director, Babylon, Center for Studies of the Multicultural Society, Tilburg University, The Netherlands.

Juliane House is Professor of Applied Linguistics, Department of General and Applied Linguistics, University of Hamburg, Germany.

Jennifer Jenkins is Senior Lecturer in Applied Linguistics , Dept of Education and Professional Studies, King's College London, UK.

Constant Leung is Professor of Educational Linguistics, Dept of Education and Professional Studies, King's College London, UK.

Martina Möllering is Senior Lecturer and Head of Department, Department of European Languages, Macquarie University, Australia.

Robert Phillipson is Research Professor, Dept of English, Copenhagen Business School, Denmark.

Julia Sallabank is a doctoral candidate, Dept of Linguistics and English Language, University of Lancaster, UK.

Pascaline Scalone is a doctoral candidate, Dept of Education and Professional Studies, King's College London, UK.

Brian Street is Professor of Language in Education, Dept of Education and Professional Studies, King's College London, UK.

Arturo Tosi is Professor of Italian Linguistics, Dept of Italian, Royal Holloway, University of London, UK.